"THESE ALL DIED IN FAITH,
NOT HAVING RECEIVED THE PROMISES,
BUT HAVING SEEN THEM AFAR OFF,
AND WERE PERSUADED OF THEM,
AND EMBRACED THEM,
AND CONFESSED THAT THEY WERE STRANGERS
AND PILGRIMS ON THE EARTH. . . ."

HEBREWS 11:13 KJV

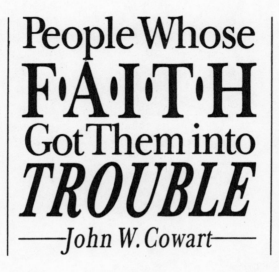

People Whose F·A·I·T·H Got Them into *TROUBLE*

—John W. Cowart—

STORIES OF COSTLY DISCIPLESHIP

INTERVARSITY PRESS
DOWNERS GROVE, ILLINOIS 60515

InterVarsity Press is the book-publishing division of InterVarsity Christian Fellowship, a student movement active on campus at hundreds of universities, colleges and schools of nursing in the United States of America, and a member movement of the International Fellowship of Evangelical Students. For information about local and regional activities, write Public Relations Dept., InterVarsity Christian Fellowship, 6400 Schroeder Rd., P.O. Box 7895, Madison, WI 53707-7895.

All Scripture quotations, unless otherwise indicated, are from the Holy Bible, New International Version. Copyright © 1973, 1978, International Bible Society. Used by permission of Zondervan Bible Publishers.

Cover illustration: John Walker

ISBN 0-8308-1737-9

Printed in the United States of America ∞

Library of Congress Cataloging-in-Publication Data

Cowart, John W.
    People whose faith got them into trouble/John W. Cowart.
      p.   cm.
    ISBN 0-8308-1737-9
    1. Christian biography. 2. Christian martyrs. I. Title.
  BR1700.2.C68 1990
  270'.092'2—dc20
    [B]   90-41336
                                          CIP

12	11	10	9	8	7	6	5	4	3	2	1
99	98	97	96	95	94	93	92	91	90		

TO GIN

Behold, thou art fair, My Love;
behold, thou art fair.
Behold, thou art fair, My Beloved;
yea, thou art pleasant.
—Song of Solomon 4:1

Author's Note

This book offers miniature portraits of a number of people who were radically different from the rest of us.

The chapters are not exhaustive biographies; they merely give glimpses of people I find to be among the most fascinating characters who have ever lived.

Some of the people told about in these pages are well known. Others you may have never heard of before. Each one exhibits certain other-worldly characteristics and values which you may find attractive, funny or odd—even repelling. Each of them acted out of place in this world, as though they were strangers here.

Each of the people in this book took up a cross and followed Jesus. He led each of them to a crucifixion. The man with the cross always leads to a crucifixion. As we take up our own crosses and follow him, we move toward our own crucifixion. We are no better than the One we follow. Why should we expect better treatment in this world than he got?

Faith *does* lead beyond trouble and pain to resurrection—eventually.

That is some consolation to the person who suffers, voluntarily or otherwise, because of faith. But crucifixion is a slow process; one nail is driven in at a time. We try to squirm away from the hammer blows. That's natural.

And resurrection does not come immediately.

So it is no surprise that at times, every one of the people I write about felt that abandoning the cross would get them out of trouble. On one level it would have. Each of these people questioned whether the faith was worth the pain.

We all do.

Yet, these people reached a decision. It was not a choice made in an air-conditioned church while the choir softly sang "Just As I Am" but a choice made while flames licked their feet, while friends condemned their decisions and while Jesus himself, with his own cross, seemed almost too far away to see anymore.

These people followed him anyhow.

They are like the rest of us only in the same way a magnet is like an ordinary horseshoe; the external appearance is the same, but some internal alignment differs.

Yet, the magnetic power of Jesus Christ remains available to everyone—even to you and me today.

You see, Jesus attracts or repels us all according to our own makeup, our own internal polarity. He works like a magnet that attracts iron with an internal molecular structure lined up with the magnetic field, or repels iron with a different polarity. The non-ferrous metals remain unaffected.

The people told about in these pages have themselves gained an attraction like an iron bar long rubbed against a magnet till the bar itself acquires the magnetic characteristics of the master lodestone. Through long and close association with Jesus, these people have become Christlike, godly . . . different.

But, there is not one of us who could not be of the same caliber as these people—if that were our choice.

But I do not choose to be like them.

You do not want to be like these people either—not really.

If you or I did, then the entire world system of things would be shaken to its very foundation.

William Law (1686-1761) said that while we praise "primitive Christians" and marvel at their deeds and piety, the only reason we are not like them is that we do not intend to be like them.

I suspect he was right.

But it is human nature to enjoy hearing about the adventures, triumphs, temptations, frustrations and failures of people we even remotely admire.

And at some time or the other in our lives, on some level (perhaps quite a shallow one) you and I feel drawn to live closer to God. We all think about it now and then and intend to—someday.

Therefore, the purpose of this book is simply to remind you of your own intentions.

John W. Cowart

THE DAY
THEY KILLED
POLYCARP

Polycarp (d. February 22, circa 166)

*T*he sound of hooves at midnight—horsemen galloping into the courtyard—and the clatter of armor as soldiers surround the house wake the old man. Two officers dismount and pound on the wooden door with the butt ends of their spears.

Maids in disheveled nightclothes rush upstairs and urge the white-haired fugitive to hide under the bed, in a closet . . . anywhere. Instead, he hushes them, drapes a cloak over his frail shoulders, descends the stairs, opens the door and invites the men who have come to arrest him inside.

He instructs the maids, "Quickly, prepare hot food and something to drink. Can't you see these men have ridden hard tonight? They need refreshment; give them the best in the house."

Confused by this unexpected reception, the arresting officers crowd into the room and cluster around a bronze charcoal brazier on the floor.

As they warm their numb hands against the cold night of February 22, 166, Polycarp, elderly bishop of Smyrna (modern-day Izmir, Turkey) makes every effort to see that his guests are comfortable. He personally serves the officers and soldiers alike from the warm dishes his maids have prepared.

His gentle manner puzzles the soldiers; they expected to find a vile, raging demon instead of a venerable man of peace and prayer. One of the men asked, "Why was so much effort made to capture such a respectable old man?"

Why indeed?

Polycarp was a Christian, and the explanation for his arrest and execution lies in the attitude of the Roman Empire toward this new religion.

Cornelius Tacitus, a Roman historian who lived from A.D. 55-120 through the reigns of nine emperors from Nero to Trajan, speaks of "a class hated for their abominations, called Christians by the populace. Christus, from whom the name had its origin, suffered the extreme penalty during the reign of Tiberius at the hands of one of our procurators, Pontius Pilatus, and a most mischievous superstition [was] thus checked for the moment." He refers to the new religion as an "evil . . . hideous and shameful" noted for its "hatred against mankind."

The *Octavius,* a book by Minucius Felix, the earliest Latin apologist for Christianity, describes what the public suspected went on in private Christian meetings. "An infant covered with meal, that it may deceive the unwary, is placed before him who is to be stained with their rites: this infant is slain by the young pupil, who has been urged on as if to harmless blows on the surface of the meal, with dark and secret wounds. Thirstily— O Horror—they lick up its blood; eagerly they divide its limbs."

No wonder Pliny the Younger, appointed governor of Bithynia by the Emperor Trajan in about A.D. 111, worried that "many people of all ages and classes and of both sexes are now being enticed into moral peril. . . . This superstition has spread like the plague, not only in the cities but in the villages and countryside as well. I feel it must be stopped."

Many wanted Christianity stopped; yet it spread. Personal contact and example rather than elaborate missionary machinery illustrated the faith to the world. Justin Martyr, a Christian apologist writing about the year A.D. 150, said, "Many changed their violent and tyrannical disposition, being overcome either by the constancy which they witnessed in the lives of their Christian neighbors, or by the extraordinary forbearance they have observed in their Christian fellow travellers when defrauded, and by the honesty of those believers with whom they have transacted business."

Business considerations also figured into the persecution of Christians. People who sold religious relics or animals for sacrifice to idols lost business whenever worshipers left their old ways to follow Christ. When Christianity was discouraged and many people returned to idol worship, business picked up again. In Saint Paul's day the silversmiths had rioted in Ephesus because their trade in souvenir replica idols was jeopardized when so many people became Christians (Acts 19:23ff). Since then and on through history many heathens have found that the suppression of Christianity causes their own financial status to prosper. For instance, after one purge of Christians, Pliny the Younger reported: "Victims for sacrifice are now everywhere on sale for which only an odd buyer could be found a short while ago." Naturally, stockmen supplying animals for use in the temples wanted Christians persecuted; they did not want to see their market drop.

Conflicting information about the Christians confused the pagans. One man reportedly exclaimed when his neighbor was led away to the arena for execution, "But he was such a good man; I never would have guessed he was a Christian!"

As official policy, a consistent stream of emperors issued edicts designed to check the sacrilege called by the Name. This created a state of affairs in which, as one ancient historian said, "the persecution of Christians was a standing matter as was that of robbers."

Pagans called the Christians "atheists" because they offered no sacrifices, had no temples and worshiped no visible god. They seemed antisocial because they refused to participate in public festivals, attend popular sports events such as gladiatorial contests, or even feast along with everyone else on religious holidays. Christians were viewed as disloyal because they refused to sacrifice to the genius of the Emperor as represented in his statues in every city. They claimed to pray *for* the emperor instead of *to* him, but this fine distinction was to the pagan mind only a subterfuge to avoid the Roman pledge of allegiance, "Caesar is Lord."

Some Christians attracted persecution to themselves.

Many acted clannish and better than other people. Others divided mankind into the saved, those who could potentially be saved, and those who were so degenerate that they would never be saved. Naturally, those lumped into the last category were annoyed. Some Christians antagonized their families and neighbors by pointing out the wickedness of others without charity or humility.

Christians sometimes rejoiced over calamities saying that fires, floods, plagues, earthquakes and such were a punishment falling on sinners who deserved no better at the hands of an angry God.

This attitude boomeranged on the Christians.

The pagans agreed that calamity came as a result of the gods being angry; but what were they angry about?

Christians!

The pagans reasoned that the very existence of Christians drew the wrath of the gods. Tertullian, a writer from Carthage who became a Christian about A.D. 190 and went on to become known as the father of Christian literature, wrote, "If the Tiber rises, if the Nile does not rise, if the heavens give no rain, if there is an earthquake, famine or pestilence, straightway the cry is 'Christianos ad Leones'—Christians to the lions."

To the pagan mind, the only way to appease the gods was to restore the person to pagan worship through sacrifice to the gods, even if the person had to be tortured or exterminated.

Even the way Christians died in the arenas drew varied interpretations from the observers. Their deaths inspired some pagans to confess the Name of Christ also. On the other hand, many pagans felt that the gods were so angry with these Christians that the deities caused them to linger on and on under torture rather than letting them find quick escape in death. As Jesus said, ". . . a time is coming when anyone who kills you will think he is offering a service to God" (Jn 16:2).

Christians caused trouble.

And Polycarp was pre-eminent among the Christians. The whole population of Smyrna acknowledged, "This is the great teacher of Asia; the Father of the Christians."

Polycarp deserved his reputation. He was the living link between the apostles and the church of his day. John, the beloved disciple, had brought Polycarp to faith in Christ, and they spent much time together when Polycarp was young. Before John's exile to Patmos he appointed Polycarp as bishop to Smyrna. At the time of his arrest, the aged Polycarp was one of the few persons still living who had actually known an apostle.

"He would speak of his familiar intercourse with John, and the rest of those who had seen the Lord. . . . He would call their words to remembrance. Whatsoever things he had heard from them respecting the Lord, both with regard to His miracles and His teaching, Polycarp, having thus received information from eyewitnesses of the Word of Life, would recount them all in harmony with the Scripture," said Irenaeus, Polycarp's pupil whom he sent to Gaul as a missionary.

Polycarp did not boast of his own association with the apostles. In his letter to the church at Philippi, he said, "I write to you concerning righteousness, not because I take anything upon myself, but because ye have invited me to do so. For neither I, nor any other such one, can come up to the wisdom of the blessed and glorified Paul. He, when among you, accurately and steadfastly taught the Word of Truth in the presence of those who were then alive."

Polycarp taught Irenaeus that "the business of the Christian is nothing else than to be ever preparing for death." He insisted that Christians are to "walk in His commandments and to love what He loved . . . not rendering evil for evil or railing for railing or blows for blows, or cursing for cursing; but being mindful of what the Lord said in His teaching." Polycarp said, "Let us be imitators of Christ's patience and if we suffer for His Name's sake let us glorify Him. For He has set us this example in Himself."

Such meekness was not only to be exhibited in the face of imminent death but also in the affairs of daily life. Polycarp's visit to the Bishop of Rome to discuss the Easter controversy illustrates this facet of his character.

The churches of Asia observed the raising of Christ from the dead on the fourteenth day of the vernal equinoctial moon, like the Jewish Passover, regardless of which day of the week it fell on; the Western churches observed Easter on the first Sunday after the first full moon following the Vernal Equinox. Thus some Christians fasted while others feasted. Neither group wished to change their custom, and feelings ran high.

Polycarp did not resolve this conflict of dates, but he did reconcile the people involved. He explained that the Scripture says we should not judge anyone with respect to meat or drink or in regard to feast days of the new moon. What good is a feast leavened with malice and contention? Why should Christians observe any exterior custom which undermines faith and love between brothers? That is more important than either the feasting or the fasting. He urged, "Loving the brotherhood and being attached to one another, joined together in truth, exhibiting the meekness of the Lord in your intercourse with one another and despising no one" is of the utmost importance. His attitude healed this serious breach between Eastern and Western churches for over a generation.

His long-cultivated humility was again demonstrated on the day of his execution.

The soldiers bundled Polycarp up in robes to protect him from the cold and mounted him on a donkey to lead him to the city stadium where the festival of *Commune Asiae,* a major occasion of Emperor worship and commemorative games, was being celebrated in Smyrna.

A recent plague and earthquake had convinced the people that the gods were angry about Christians existing in the city. Therefore, a number of Christians were being given the opportunity to declare "Caesar is Lord" and sacrifice to his image, or else be tortured to death.

Some of the Christians were beaten with whips until "their bellies popped open exposing their innards." Others were pressed into a bed of spikes till pierced through and left writhing on display around the stadium.

A young Christian noble named Germanicus fought off the wild beasts so heroically that the proconsul, Statius Quadratus, had the animals leashed and offered the youth another chance, reasoning, "You are too young to waste the good life ahead of you. If you'll just deny this Christ you can live."

Germanicus deliberately provoked the lion, seizing its mane and drawing it to him. The cat bit into his shoulder, unsheathed its claws and set its hind legs churning.

In contrast to Germanicus, consider Quintus, a Phrygian, who had approached the proconsul and voluntarily put himself forward as a Christian.

When he saw the lion enter the arena, he cowered. His courage left him. He ran to the spot beneath the proconsul's box. There he cringed, begging for his life. He denied Christ, swore that Caesar is Lord, publicly sacrificed to the image . . . and lived.

Their appetites whetted by this triumph of paganism, the crowd in the stands began chanting, "Away with the atheists! Away with the atheists! Let Polycarp be sought out!"

The Irenarch, the district peace officer whose name was Herod, dispatched troops to bring in Polycarp on the night before the final day of the celebration.

Upon hearing the Bishop was in custody, the Irenarch and his father hurried to meet the escorting soldiers on the road. They took the aged prisoner into their chariot and tried to reason with him. "What harm is there in just saying Lord Caesar?" they questioned.

"I shall never do what you desire of me," Polycarp insisted. At that, they shoved him out of the moving chariot, dislocating his hip.

Perhaps, as he hobbled the rest of the way into the city where the morning crowd was already gathering at the stadium, he recalled the words Christ addressed to the messenger of Smyrna in Revelation 2:8-10; after all he was the Bishop of Smyrna and John, who had appointed him to that position, recorded these words: ". . . Do not be afraid of what you are about to suffer. . . . Be faithful, even to the point of death, and I will give you the crown of life."

The Irenarch hauled Polycarp before the proconsul, who also tried to reason with him. "Respect your old age. You've had a good life; why end it like this? Live out your remaining days in peace and security. Swear by the genius of Caesar; if you'll utter just one little word against Christ, I'll release you."

Polycarp straightened up under the weight of his chains, which he called "the only fitting ornament for believers," and clearly announced for all the crowd to hear, "Eighty and six years have I served Him and He never did me any injury: How then can I blaspheme My King who saved me? . . . Hear my free confession—I am a Christian."

His words enraged the mob.

"I have wild beasts," the proconsul threatened.

"Call for them," Polycarp said. "I am unalterably resolved not to change from good to evil."

"If beasts don't scare you, I have fire."

"Your fire burns only for a short time then flickers out; but you are ignorant of the Judgment to come of everlasting fire prepared for the wicked."

The proconsul summoned the stadium announcer. Trumpets blew. The announcer proclaimed from the center of the arena three times as prescribed by law, "Polycarp has confessed himself a Christian."

At this proclamation, the mob swarmed out of the stands and into streets surrounding the stadium. Shoving and trampling each other, they surged through shops, baths and private homes snatching up floorboards, hitching posts, furniture . . . anything that would burn.

Back into the arena they rushed, heaping combustible things around the saint who prayed, "I bless thee for having been pleased in thy goodness to bring me to this hour."

The executioner threw a torch on the pile. An eyewitness

said, "The flame billowed like an arch, like the wind-filled sail of a ship. . . . He appeared within, not like flesh which is charred, but as bread that is baked."

The executioner mutilated the corpse. The proconsul ordered it completely cremated to keep Christians from recovering even calcified bones. Still ignorant of the nature of Christian faith, he said that he did this "lest forsaking him that was crucified, they begin to worship this one instead."

The pagans did not understand, said the anonymous Christian eyewitness to these things, "that we can never forsake Christ, nor adore any other, though we love the martyrs as His disciples and imitators, for the great love they bore for their Master and King. . . .

"The martyrdom of holy Polycarp was on the second day of the month of Xanticus, on the seventh day before the Kalends of March, on the great Sabbath, at the eighth hour. He was arrested by Herod, in the high-priesthood of Philip of Tralles, in the proconsulate of Statius Quadratus, in the everlasting reign of Jesus Christ."

THE MAN BEHIND SANTA CLAUS

Nicholas of Myra (d. December 6, circa 343)

*F*ather, Father, wake up! There's a man climbing the lattice beside our window," the girl cried.

The weary father shook off sleep. He stumbled, half-awake, to his daughters' bedroom and peeked out the window. Someone was stealthily climbing the lattice.

"Now what? As if I didn't have troubles enough already," said the father. "I'll fix this rascal." He picked up a hefty length of firewood from beside the hearth and crept outside.

The troubled father had spent a restless night. When he lay down, his mind kept skipping from problem to problem. Three marriageable daughters and no dowry to offer even one prospective groom! Poverty had sapped his resources. He had decided to sell the girls to a local brothel. That appeared to be the only way out. But he was dissatisfied with his decision, and sleep eluded him.

Now this!

As he opened the door, he heard a thud. The intruder had thrown something into the girls' room and was now scurrying down the lattice.

The angry father pursued the running intruder. Soon they both collapsed, panting against a rock wall. The father, too tired from the chase to lift his cudgel, saw that the intruder was only a breathless adolescent boy.

The eldest daughter came running up. "Look, Father," she exclaimed, "Look what he threw in our window." She held out a leather bag stuffed with gold coins.

"What is the meaning of this?" demanded the father.

His captive explained that he was a Christian and that his parents had died recently, leaving him an inheritance. The young man explained:

> The Lord said that we should sell what we have and give to the poor, then follow him. I want to follow Jesus, so when I learned of your problem and what you planned to do . . . what else could I do? If a man has anything of this world's goods and sees a brother in need and hardens his heart against his brother and does not give, then how can the love of God abide in such a man?

The puzzled father, still suspecting a trick, asked, "Why did you sneak up to our house at night? What are you really up to? What is your name?"

The boy replied, "My name is Nicholas. I came secretly because Jesus commanded that when you give to the poor, you shouldn't let your left hand know what your right hand does; keep your giving a secret. Keep the money, Sir, but I beg one favor in return; don't let anyone know about this. Keep it a secret."

The father promised and for years did not disclose how he got his daughters' dowry.

This story, told by Metaphrastes, a Greek bishop who published his book, *The Acts of Nicholas,* in A.D. 912, reveals one reason why St. Nicholas, the historical person on whom the legend of Santa Claus is based, is one of the world's most popular figures. *The Acts of Nicholas,* written about 600 years after the fact, is the oldest documentary evidence of the Nicholas legend.

Nicholas was born in the third century in Patras, a city in Asia Minor. His wealthy parents were devout Christians. When they died, he used his inheritance to help the poor and entered the Monastery of Holy Sion, near the city of Myra, to get an education.

When he came of age, Nicholas made a life-changing trip to the Holy Land.

He went to Bethlehem to see the spot of the Nativity. He stood on the Mount of Olives where Christ had taught. He visited Golgotha where Jesus died on the cross. And he prayed in the empty tomb from which Jesus had risen. This pilgrimage confirmed in his mind what he had studied in the Scripture: that Christ was indeed Emmanuel, God-with-us. This settled conviction shaped his future career.

As he sailed home, his ship ran into a storm. Nicholas helped the sailors in the rigging and took over the tiller. The sailors attributed their survival to him; he attributed safety to God. He vowed to go to church to offer thanks as soon as the vessel reached land.

While Nicholas was on his pilgrimage, the bishop of Myra had died. The church leaders disagreed about who should fill the office. After a lengthy debate, one suggested, "We'll let God decide; the first man who comes through the church doors tomorrow morning will be the new bishop."

Nicholas's ship docked at dawn.

Immediately he went to give thanks for deliverance from the storm. The church leaders greeted him at the door with miter and staff of office. Thus, according to legend, he became one of the youngest bishops in history. Some sources indicate he was still a teen-ager when he took office.

It was not long before Bishop Nicholas came into conflict with government authorities. A famine descended on Myra. Crops withered in the fields. No food was to be found anywhere. His people looked to Nicholas to save them from starvation. Eustathios, the provincial prefect, commandeered several cargo ships loaded with grain riding at anchor in the harbor at Andriaki. This corrupt official planned to hold the grain until scarcity forced prices to their highest. Nicholas revealed the governor's hoarding and shamed him into releasing the shipment.

Nicholas further aggravated Eustathios when he learned of the proposed execution of three political prisoners. Nicholas argued for the release of these innocent men.

"Too late," Eustathios cried. "They're on the way to the chopping block now."

Nicholas rushed to the town square where the executions were to take place. The first prisoner lay with his neck on the block, his head over the basket.

The executioner swung.

Nicholas grabbed the sword as it descended, snatching it out of the executioner's hands. He cut the prisoners' bonds and set them free. Public acclaim assured the men's continued safety. The governor backed down—for a while.

On February 23, A.D. 303, the Emperor Diocletian issued an edict which launched one of the most systematic and prolonged persecutions the Christian church has ever endured.

The Diocletian persecution marks one of the first organized

attacks on the Scriptures, for the edict demanded that Christians turn in their holy books to be burned. To refuse meant death. The faithful (such as Felix, bishop of Thibiuca, who told the arresting officers, "It is better for me to be burned than the divine Scriptures") resorted to various subterfuges, such as turning in grammar books, medical books, collections of sermons and other religious books to protect the Scriptures. These actions forced the Christians to clearly define which writings should be considered divinely inspired and which should not.

Strangers confiscated property owned by Christians. The situation repeated the outrages reported in a letter by Dionysius, bishop of Alexandria, a few years earlier when mobs "rushed to the houses of Christians, breaking in on those who were known as neighbours, and looted and plundered. The more valuable property they stole; the cheaper wooden articles were strewn about the streets and burnt, so that the city looked as if it had been taken by an enemy. But the believers . . . took joyfully the spoiling of their goods."

Eusebius, an eyewitness, said:

Words cannot describe the outrageous agonies endured by the martyrs. . . . They were torn to bits from head to foot with potsherds like claws, till death released them. Women were tied by one foot and hoisted high in the air, head downwards, their bodies completely naked without a morsel of clothing. . . .

I was in these places and saw many of the executions myself. . . . The orgy went on so long that the murderous blade became blunt and killed by its weight. The executioners themselves became exhausted and took turns at the work.

Relatively few Christians dramatized their faith with stirring last words before an audience in the arena; for most, the fear, the anxiety, the uncertainty, the hiding, the imprisonment and the anguish went on for years and years. Christian children grew up knowing no conditions other than these.

Like many others, Bishop Nicholas was caught early in the persecution and imprisoned. They beat him. They branded his skin. They used iron pliers to pinch various parts of his body. Then he was left alone in his cell till his wounds healed enough for the process to begin all over again. The persecution kept up for years. Yet Nicholas would not deny that Jesus is very God of very God.

At the height of the persecution, a plague broke out. Fearing contagion, pagans dumped members of their own families in the streets when they got sick. But Christians, Eusebius said, "heedless of the danger, took charge of the sick, attending to their every need and ministering to them . . . drawing on themselves the sickness of their neighbors. . . . The best of our brothers lost their lives in this manner . . . so death in this form, the result of great piety and strong faith, seems in every way the equal of martyrdom."

When the plague passed, the pagans resumed the persecution with renewed vigor. Judges "made a show of cruelty . . . and in a wretched competition for new tortures attempted to best their rival judges as if they were striving for a prize."

They sentenced young Christian girls to be chained naked in brothels for the use of any passerby.

The pagan emperor died. Constantine assumed the throne and stopped the persecution.

Nicholas had endured the torture, but now he confronted a more insidious danger threatening to undermine Christianity.

Arius, a popular Alexandrian preacher, began teaching that Christ was inferior to God. He taught that Jesus was not God-become-man, but rather an intermediate spirit creature which was "enfleshed"— neither God nor even quite human.

Arius spread his ideas by setting them to the music of drinking songs which were popular at pagan orgies. His most well-known song, disparaging the Incarnation and birth of Christ, was "Thalia." It bordered on the obscene, but the tune was so catchy that soon virtually everyone was whistling it in the streets and markets.

"So scandalous did the situation become that in the very theaters of the unbelievers the venerable teachings of God were exposed to the most shameful ridicule," said Eusebius.

Confessors who had survived the persecution as Nicholas had preached and reasoned with the people about Jesus, pointing to such Scriptures as:

For in Christ all the fullness of the Deity lives in bodily form. (Col 2:9)

Anyone who has seen me has seen the Father. (Jn 14:9)

The Word became flesh and made his dwelling among us. (Jn 1:14)

The Son is the radiance of God's glory and the exact representation of his being. (Heb 1:3)

All this doctrine was to no avail. Arianism appealed to minds which reasoned that since they could not understand the Trinity, there could be no Trinity.

Constantine called a council of church leaders at Nicaea to discuss whether or not Jesus is really God, the teachings of Arius, and other matters dividing the church.

Those attending the Council of Nicaea had survived the Diocletian Persecution. A number of them concealed the stubs of lost limbs. Many were hamstrung. (Prisoners in the mines were crippled in this way to keep them from escaping.) Many had empty sockets where their tormentors had gouged out eyes.

Legend has it that in the course of his presentation to the Council, Arius began to sing the "Thalia." Some of the bishops rushed out of the meeting. Others covered their ears. St. Nicholas walked slowly to the center of the floor where Arius sang—and deliberately punched him in the mouth!

The shocked bishops sympathized with Nicholas but could not condone his action. After all, the Christ whom Nicholas defended was he who taught his followers to love their enemies and be people of peace.

They deprived Nicholas of his bishopric (he was later restored to office) and they expelled Arius. Before the Council ended, they wrote the Nicene Creed which states what most Christians believe about Jesus. No other document which Nicholas may have helped write remains.

Nicholas spent the rest of his life in Myra caring for the sick, founding orphanages and protecting the poor from exploiters. He was noted for playing with children and scandalized his more dignified contemporaries by letting street urchins wear his bishop's hat.

Nicholas died on December 6 around A.D. 343; but his love for Jesus, his defense of the Christmas doctrine of the Incarnation and his habit of generous secret giving, all combine to cause his shadow to linger in the legendary figure of Santa Claus.

HE DID
NOT WANT
TO GO

Patrick of Ireland (d. March 17, circa 461)

Magnus Sucatus Patricius traveled to Ireland twice. He went once because of Irish pirates; he went the second time because of God. He did not want to go either time.

His first visit came at a time of great turmoil in Europe. The empire was crumbling. For 470 years Roman legions had controlled Britain, holding back the barbarians and spreading Roman law, living standards and culture. While Roman garrisons manned the walls built across the island to separate civilized Britain from the Picts and the Scots, Roman ships thronged the harbors, bringing the goods of the Empire to Britain.

Roman roads spanned the countryside. Roman baths, theaters and aqueducts graced the cities. But by A.D. 385, hostile barbarians, the Huns and the Goths, in other parts of the empire, forced Rome to withdraw her troops, leaving British citizens to defend themselves.

The last legion sailed from Britain in A.D. 400, and immediately the Norse, the Caledonians, the Saxons, and the Irish began to ravish the formerly protected towns and estates. Roving bands raped, looted and captured slaves for sale in their homelands.

Irish pirates crept along the coast in *curraghs,* wicker framework boats covered with stitched cowhides. These lightweight boats were perfect for coastal raids. Powered by twelve oarsmen, the shallow-drafted *curraghs* could sneak up the estuaries silently for pre-dawn attacks.

Patrick's father was a deacon of the Christian church and a *decurion,* a local official of the national government. He was also a minor member of the nobility and owned a seaside villa which was particularly vulnerable to pirate raids.

The attack came when Patrick was sixteen.

Screaming barbarians charged up the slope from the sea, hacking down startled defenders and casting nets over fleeing victims. Although his parents and the rest of his family escaped, Patrick and many of his father's servants were captured, bound and thrust into the bottom of a pirate boat to wallow in the bilge water as the raid continued along the coast.

Saint Patrick was on his way to Ireland for the first time.

In Ireland Patrick was sold as a slave to Miliucc of Slemich, a Druid tribal chieftain who put the boy to work herding pigs. Patrick felt lost and helpless; he had gone from nobleman's heir to swineherd overnight. Slavery beat pride and dignity out of him. He had no chance for education, no friends, no possessions, no name, no hope.

He labored in filth and squalor among the animals. Finally, deprived of every human consolation, he turned to God. In his book *Confessions,* he wrote, "I was sixteen and knew not the true

God but in a strange land the Lord opened my unbelieving eyes, and I was converted."

Patrick gives few details, but apparently his memory of Christian teachings he had learned as a child resulted in his conversion.

The new convert spent much time in the presence of the Lord and eventually came to thank God for his captivity as an opportunity to know Christ. He became convinced that his slave state was a gift from God, so he served his barbarian master well, laboring as unto the Lord. He said, "Anything that happens to me, whether pleasant or distasteful, I ought to accept it with equanimity giving thanks to God . . . who never disappoints."

Patrick learned to pray as he worked or walked or rested. He said, "Love and reverence for God came to me more and more, building up my faith so much that daily I would pray a hundred times or more. Even while working in the woods or on the mountain, I woke up to pray before dawn. . . . Now I understand that it was the fervent Spirit praying within me."

His devotion to God earned him the teasing nickname "Holy-Boy" among his fellow slaves. He remained a slave of the Druid for six years. Then came escape.

One night as he lay sleeping, Patrick heard a voice in a dream telling him, "Wake up. Your ship is waiting for you." He sneaked away and struggled through two hundred miles of hostile territory to the coast where he found a *curragh* "of more than one hide" preparing to sail.

The captain refused passage to the runaway slave, but as Patrick walked away praying, one of the crew called him back to the ship. After an arduous voyage and near starvation, he arrived home. "Again I was in Britain with my people who welcomed me as their son," he wrote.

In his own mind Patrick was through with Ireland and the

Irish. At twenty-two, he had many opportunities before him: He could continue his education, catch up with his social life, assume his responsibilities as heir of a nobleman.

Little is known about this time in his life. Patrick may have studied in France or Italy; he may have entered the priesthood at this time. He does not tell us. The next event he relates in *Confessions* is how God called him to return to Ireland.

He wrote, "I did not go back to Ireland of my own accord. It is not in my own nature to show divine mercy toward the very ones who once enslaved me."

Concerning his return to Ireland as a missionary he wrote, "It was the furthest thing from me, but God made me fit, causing me to care about and labour for the salvation of others."

This change of attitude toward his mission came in part as the result of another dream. He saw a messenger named Victoricus coming across the sea from Ireland bearing letters labeled "The Voice of the Irish."

When Patrick began to read these letters he thought he heard the people in the Wood of Focluth, where he had been a slave, crying out to him, saying, "Holy-Boy, we beg you, come walk among us again."

He awoke knowing he had to go back.

Patrick still faced three major obstacles: his family, because they wanted him to stay home; the clergy, because they thought the Irish were not worth saving; and finances, because he wanted to pay his own way. His *Confessions* reveals how God dealt with each hindrance.

"Since I was home at last having suffered such hardship, my family pleaded with me not to leave," he said. They were justly alarmed. As an escaped slave, he faced horrible retribution. The Druids were known to weave criminals and runaway slaves into giant wicker baskets and suspend them over a fire to roast alive.

Patrick often lovingly mentions his family, which had survived the pirate raid, and he refers to the pain of leaving it again. He said, "Leaving my home and family was a costly price to pay; but afterwards, I received a more valuable thing: the gift of knowing and loving God."

"Many friends tried to stop my mission. They said, 'Why does this fellow waste himself among dangerous enemies who don't even know God?' "

These churchmen considered the Irish to be barbaric enemies not worth saving. But Patrick attributes a more worthy motive to his detractors: "Their objection was not due to malice. The project just didn't appeal to them. I believe it was because I am so uncouth."

His lack of education bothered Patrick all his life, and he often apologizes for it in his writings.

Because Patrick believed his enemies were worth saving, he could later say, "Once the Irish worshipped idols and unclean things, having no knowledge of the True God, but now they are among God's own people. Even the children of their kings are numbered among the monks and virgins of Christ."

Patrick insisted on paying his own way. He wanted to give what was his and not what belonged to other people.

He said, "Contrary to the desires of my seniors, when supporters offered me gifts, I refused to accept them, thus offending the contributors. . . . Some devout women pressed me with gifts, even offering their jewelry, but I returned these love-offerings to them. They were also offended. The reason I acted thus was to demonstrate prudence in everything. . . . I did not want to give the unbelievers even the smallest thing to criticize."

But if he refused to accept financial help from church or friends, how could he finance his endeavor? He said, "I was born free, the son of a *decurion;* but I sold my title of nobility— there is no shame nor regret in this—in order to become the slave of Christ serving this barbaric nation."

Patrick used his inheritance money to purchase a boat and finance his mission. He and his party sailed back to Ireland in A.D. 432. Landing at the port of Inver Dea, they were welcomed by a rock-throwing mob.

They sailed along the coast of Ireland, landing and preaching along the way. Patrick preached at isolated farms, to hostile crowds on the beaches, to women and children drawing water at country wells.

At one farm, tradition tells us, Patrick came upon an old man who was dying. Patrick sought to comfort him and lead him to salvation in Christ. The invalid argued for his old way of life. Finally Patrick asked him, "Why are you grasping at a life which is even now failing you? Why do you neglect to prepare for the life to come?"

The old man pondered the questions. Then he repented, believed and was baptized. He eventually recovered from his illness and became one of Patrick's staunchest followers. As Christianity became more established Patrick assigned this man, whose name was Ros, the task of codifying Ireland's laws, bringing them into conformity with Christian belief and morality.

Patrick's attempts at evangelism were not always so successful. He returned to Slemich to confront his former owner with the claims of Christ. Rather than forsake his heathen gods, Miliuce sealed himself inside his house and set it afire. The Druid drowned out Patrick's pleadings with screamed curses and invocations to his gods. He cremated himself and all his possessions.

Patrick traveled over the Irish countryside in a chariot, spreading the gospel and bringing with it social reform and a written alphabet. He conducted open-air schools to teach his converts to read and write.

Until this time, writing was the jealously guarded secret of Druid wizards who used the Ogram script to inscribe pillars of stone. But Patrick believed in educating his converts to read the Scripture.

A clash with the Druids was inevitable.

The religion of the Druids was firmly entrenched in Ireland. They worshiped and tried to appease manifold spirits in the guise of stones, trees, storms and the sun. They may have constructed megalithic monuments similar to Stonehenge to aid in their style of astrology.

Druid sorcerers claimed to be able to control weather, so it was important for them to be aware of celestial changes. One of their most important rites occurred at the vernal equinox when the sun begins its return to warm the Northern Hemisphere. In A.D. 433, the vernal equinox fell on March 26, Easter Sunday. Patrick chose that day to challenge the wizards.

At the time Ireland was a loose confederation of warlords under High King Leary. They all met to seek the blessing of the Druids on the vernal equinox at a hill called Tara.

In order to call the sun back to the north, the Druid custom was to extinguish all fires in the kingdom. The chief wizard then ignited a bonfire as part of the ritual. Then runners bearing firebrands raced through the fields carrying new fire to each village. Thus the Druids showed that it was their enchantments which brought warmth back to the hearths of the nation.

On the night of the ceremony, as the warlords and wizards worshiped in the darkness of their great stone circle, there was a huge bonfire already burning on the hill opposite their megalith. Patrick had lit a blazing Paschal fire this Easter to commemorate Christ, the Light of the World.

The Druids were outraged. They dispatched troops to bring Patrick to the council and demanded an explanation for his blasphemy. Patrick spoke to them on the nature of the Trinity, the mystery of the Incarnation and the triumph of Christ's resurrection.

Some believed. Others attempted to kill him.

Legend colors this encounter with many fantastic incidents, including the burning of one of Patrick's followers in a wicker bower as a human sacrifice by the Druids. No matter what actually happened that night, Patrick became a national figure, and his controversial message was discussed everywhere.

Patrick believed that he was living in the last days before Christ's return and that the Lord deserved to be worshiped by men from every nation, even the barbaric Irish. So he felt responsible "to preach the Gospel to the edge of the earth beyond which no man lives." He says that Christ called his people to be fishers of men. "Therefore, we must spread a wide net so we can catch a teeming multitude for God."

Patrick's sense of gratitude to God for creating and saving him permeates his writings. "I was an illiterate slave, as ignorant as one who neglects to provide for his future. And I am certain of this: that although I was as a dumb stone lying squashed in the mud, the Mighty and Merciful God came, dug me out and set me on top of the wall. Therefore, I praise Him and ought to render Him something for His wonderful benefits to me both now and in eternity," he wrote.

This gratitude and burning love for Christ drove Patrick to challenge heathenism wherever he found it. He entered the stockades of the warlords, preaching to hostile warriors dressed in strips of fur or naked with their bodies painted with blue clay and scarred with whorling tattoos.

He crisscrossed Ireland in his chariot. He visited the waddle huts of slaves, bearing comfort and hope. He even preached at the racetracks, converting men in the midst of gambling, drinking and orgies. Thousands of Irishmen were converted through his relentless evangelism, motivated by loving gratitude.

He not only preached but ministered to the whole person, bringing a gospel which raised the standard of life for the Irish. He paid judges' salaries out of his own pocket so they could judge impartially rather than depend on a reward from the person who won a suit. He founded monasteries which survived as centers of learning till the age of the Vikings.

Having been a slave himself, he was concerned with the plight of slaves. He wrote, "The women who live in slavery suffer greatly. They endure terror and are constantly threatened. Their masters forbid these maidens to follow Christ, but He gives them grace to follow bravely."

Although Patrick was compassionate in his preaching and conscientious in his social programs, on occasion he demonstrated a fiery, scathing indignation.

After his ministry was established in one of the coastal towns, Patrick baptized a large group of converts. Shortly after the ceremony, the town was raided by soldiers of King Coroticus, a nominal Christian king from Britain.

The raiders slaughtered the men and children. The good-looking young women, still dressed in white baptismal gowns, were captured to sell to a brothel in Scotland.

Patrick was furious.

He fired off a scorching protest to the people of Coroticus, excommunicating the perpetrators of this "horrible, unspeakable crime" and demanded restoration of the hostages. He wrote:

The Church mourns in anguish not over the slain but over those carried off to a far away land for the purpose of gross, open sin. Think of it! Christians made slaves by Christians! Sold to serve the lusts of wicked pagan Picts!

I don't know who to cry for the most; the ones murdered, the ones captured, or the agents of the devil who did this— because they will be slaves in the everlasting torment of Hell.

Because of his stands for righteousness, Patrick suffered insult and persecution. The Druids often tried to poison him. Once a barbarian warrior speared his chariot driver to death, thinking he was killing Patrick.

Patrick was often ambushed during his evangelistic tours, and at least once he was enslaved again for a short time. He sometimes had to purchase safe passage through a hostile warlord's territory in order to continue his mission. He wrote, "Every day I expect to be murdered or robbed or enslaved; but I'm not afraid of these things because of the promises of Heaven."

Patrick faced opposition not only from nominal Christians, pagan warlords and Druid wizards, but from his church as well. Ecclesiastical authorities in Britain questioned his fitness to be a bishop and held a hearing at which he was not present and at which his dearest friend spoke against him. The records are murky, but it is possible that for a time he was suspended or placed on probation, and his convert Benigus, a former tribal warlord, may have succeeded him as bishop of Ireland.

At the time a controversy concerning Pelagianism was brewing between churchmen in Britain and on the Continent. (Pelagius in Britain had taught that men could live good lives and by their own free will win salvation.) Although Patrick in his writings does not dwell on church bickering, it appears that he may have been a victim of the power struggle between the factions involved.

The most important result of this crisis in his life was that it prompted him to write his *Confessions,* which, along with a hymn and his letter to the people of Coroticus, comprise the only surviving records of his life and thoughts.

Near the conclusion of his *Confessions* he wrote, "The only reason I had to return to the people I once barely escaped from was the Gospel and its promises."

Patrick preached the gospel and its promises to "the edge of the world beyond which no man dwells," and speaking to his readers he advised, "I wish that you also would exert greater effort and begin more powerful acts for God."

A New Kind of Simpleton

Francis of Assisi (d. October 3, 1226)

*U*ntil the day he stripped himself naked on the church steps, no one in the Italian village of Assisi considered Francesco Bernardone crazy.

Before February 5, 1207, everyone assumed that he was a normal, if high-spirited, young man. There were hardly any indications that he was turning into some kind of fool.

Francesco was the son of Pieto Bernardone, a successful cloth merchant, a fact the boy naturally took advantage of to appropriate the finest materials for his own clothes.

He enjoyed good company and surrounded himself with sparkling friends. Together, they sang popular troubadour tunes, drank, feasted, chased nubile wenches, pulled sophomoric pranks on stable citizens, and spent Daddy's cash on any whim.

This medieval fraternity called their club "The Gay Brigade" and lived up to their motto, "By wits or by fists." When their actions crossed more than the boundaries of good taste and aggravated the authorities, someone's daddy crossed the appropriate palms, and the trouble was dismissed. And the boys, who sported such nicknames as Heartbreaker, Darling, Fairflower or Courteous, went back to their reveling.

Francesco, nicknamed Frenchy the Chief, relished the ideals of romantic chivalry. His ambition was to gain renown as a knight—winning his spurs, slaying infidels and wooing pale maidens.

Soon his chance came.

Assisi declared war on the neighboring Italian town of Perugia.

Francesco's father outfitted him for war—shining armor, a war charger, a plumed helmet, a slender lance, an oil-tempered sword.

Resplendent in this knightly uniform, the future Saint Francis rode to the battle. He was promptly captured by the enemy, which took his armor and threw him in jail.

His daddy ransomed him, and The Gay Brigade welcomed him back to Assisi as a war hero.

Again his father bought him new equipment and even supplied him with a page-boy. And again he left to win the spurs of knighthood. His friends gave him another lavish send-off party.

This time he never even made it to the front.

Francis returned home for no apparent reason. He began to act different. He gave away his armor. Everyone knew something had happened to him.

Some speculated that perhaps he was ill or had fallen in love. Others scoffed that he had simply chickened out.

Many whispered that it was a shame for such a promising

young man to be afflicted . . . to be *rimbambito* (re-babyfied).

What happened?

On the road near Assisi stood the Leper Hospital of San Salvatore administered by the Order of Crugigeri, and as Francis had ridden forth to battle, he met a leper.

Historian Anthony Mockler, who wrote *Francis of Assisi: The Wandering Years,* described what is now known as Hansen's disease:

Leprosy in its severest form spreads rapidly affecting both the skin and the nerves. Ulcerations appear first on the little fingers, then on all the joints of hands and feet, leading eventually to the dropping-off of fingers and toes. Nodules the size of walnuts affect the face, thickening the nose and lips, chin, cheeks and ears. Motor paralysis sets in. The muscles of the face are contracted and distorted by atrophy; ectopia of the lower lids prevents the leper from shutting his eyes. . . . The leper suffers from unquenchable thirst. . . . The skin shrinks; hair, teeth and nails fall off—but the mind is unaffected.

When the fledgling knight saw such a man on the road, he urged his horse to gallop faster beyond the disgusting specter.

But as Francis galloped by, he suddenly recognized Christ in the guise of "the least of these my brethren."

Francis stopped. He dismounted and gave the leper alms. He kissed the contorted face, seated the man on the war charger and walked, leading the horse, to the leper's destination.

In his testament, written years later, Francis says this of the incident:

When I was in sin, the sight of lepers nauseated me beyond measure; But then God himself led me into their company, and I had pity on them. When I had once become acquainted with them, what had previously nauseated me became a source of spiritual and physical consolation for me. After that

I did not wait long before leaving the world.
At first, his leaving the world consisted of washing the sores of lepers and praying in deserted country chapels.

In one ruined church, as he prayed, Francis envisioned Christ writhing in agony on the cross for our sin. The crucified Jesus looked at him and said, "Repair my house which, as you see, is falling into ruin."

Francis assumed God wanted him to rebuild the dilapidated chapel. He was so sure God meant the physical maintenance of the church that from then on he always found a broom and swept any church he passed.

Rebuilding churches costs money. Francis looked for income where he always had before; he blithely went to his father's warehouse, grabbed a few bolts of the finest cloth, sold them for quick cash and took the money to the chapel.

Pietro Bernardone had patiently supported his son's former lifestyle but balked at financing religious fanaticism. He had his son locked up for a while, testing his sanity. Exasperated, he finally sued Francis in ecclesiastical court to get the money back. The whole town gathered on the church steps to witness this trial before the bishop.

The frustrated father disowned his eccentric son. In turn, Francis renounced all right to his expected inheritance. He not only gave back the money but stripped off all his clothing made of his father's cloth and flung it at Pietro's feet.

His father had had enough. He snatched up money and clothes and left his son standing naked on the church steps.

The shocked bishop swirled his own cloak over Francis for modesty's sake, then hurried him inside the church and gave him rags from the poor box to wear.

Francis strolled away from Assisi singing a happy troubadour ballad. On his way back to his ruined chapel in the woods, two bandits jumped out of the bushes to rob him. Finding him penniless, they got mad and stuck him headfirst in a snow-filled ditch.

But the determined man's commission to "rebuild my church" remained. He needed building materials. Over the following months, Francis began singing hymns and popular troubadour ballads on many of the street corners of Assisi. He refused to accept money for his music; he would only take building stones. When he had earned a few bricks with his tunes, he shouldered them and trudged up the mountain to set them in the wall.

People watched.

They called him "Pazzo!"—madman. They began to pity him. Some began to help him carry up stones. A mason donated mortar. A few helped him build. They sang along with him. The Chapel of San Damiano was rebuilt!

Soon twelve men from all stations of life had renounced the world's value system and joined Francis in following Jesus without reservation. They ordered their life by the words of Christ: "As you go, preach this message: 'The kingdom of heaven is near.' Heal the sick, raise the dead, cleanse those who have leprosy, drive out demons. Freely you have received, freely give. Do not take along any gold or silver or copper in your belts; take no bag for the journey, or extra tunic, or sandals or a staff; for the worker is worth his keep" (Mt 10:7-10).

Francis and his men went about telling about Christ and his passion in the Italian language, not ecclesiastical Latin. Latin was the language of the educated, while the common people spoke vernacular Italian, and Francis and his disciples wanted to communicate with everyone.

To do this, they determined to own nothing whatsoever; each sold everything he owned and gave the cash raised to poor families. They tended sick folk, played with children and helped farmers in the fields, refusing all pay other than food for that single day. Leftovers were shared with beggars or scattered for wild birds.

When they could earn no food, they begged from door to door. They slept in the open on the ground and dressed in rags as penitents.

Christians were strengthened, worldlings converted and the established clergy awed by these first Franciscans who teasingly named themselves *Joculatores Domini,* God's Jugglers.

Some clergy suspected that this radical Christianity savored of some undefined heresy; surely God does not condone irresponsible, foolish behavior, does he?

Feeling the need for official sanction, Francis walked to Rome to see Pope Innocent III.

In his tattered beggar's robes, Francis strolled blithely past Vatican guards and buttoned-holed the pope in a private garden. The pope kicked him out saying, "Such as you are more suited to preach to pigs than people; go wallow with them."

Francis hiked to the nearest pigsty and wallowed with pigs in the mire praising God. Caked with pig filth, he re-entered the Vatican, again encountered the pope and said, "I have obeyed your command; now . . ."

The pope was impressed.

He approved Francis' request. Soon hundreds of people joined one of the three branches of the Friars Minor, the official title given the Franciscans.

As missionaries, they traveled to Spain, England, Germany and Moslem lands. They preached at markets, at horse races, at jousting tournaments and in churches—and they swept the church after delivering the sermon.

They gathered annually at their headquarters, Portiuncula, near Assisi, to report what God had done, to pray and to plan their next mission.

Once, according to legend, as the Friars prayed with Francis, people from Assisi rushed up the mountain with fire-fighting equipment; they said the mountain was aglow. They thought a forest fire endangered the praying men. There was no fire.

At the General Meeting in 1218, seeing that Francis had made no physical provision for the gathering of over 3,000 men, a visiting cleric questioned, "Could faith be so naively simple?"

Francis answered, "I may speak as a fool, but faith that is not simple can never move a feather, let alone a mountain. . . . 'Be not anxious for your life, what ye shall eat or what ye shall drink.' . . . The Heavenly Father can be trusted to the limit— to the limit and beyond."

Right then, horse carts began appearing from every direction on the plain, winding their way toward the mountain, all loaded with food from various cities, all delivered unasked for.

At one of these meetings, everyone agreed that thirty missionaries ought to go to pagan Germany. But which thirty? Francis called a little boy who was visiting and told the child to pick any thirty men. The child selected the men, and they immediately started walking north. Their mission proved successful.

Francis yearned to reach Moslems who were generally feared and scorned by Christians. Pope Honorius III had mounted a crusade led by John of Briene. Through a series of mishaps, Christian infighting and military strategy, the Crusader Army wandered south of the Holy Land and in August of 1218 had been laying siege to Damietta, Egypt, for eighteen months. Francis went there.

He found the Christian army whoring after camp followers, squabbling in factions, looting, gambling, raping, drinking and stealing, while their leaders jockeyed for pre-eminence and undercut each other's efforts.

Francis ministered to the wounded and preached God's

peace to the soldiers. The leaders resented him, called him a traitor and accused him of undermining morale.

Before one assault on the city, various factions of clergy were boasting about their divine call. One claimed, "I am called to exterminate the Saracens." Another exulted, "I'm presently called as the pre-eminent Papal Legate." Francis said in turn, "The Lord told me he wished me to be a new kind of simpleton."

On August 29, the Crusaders surged across the moat to the city's triple ring of walls. Casting up grappling hooks and scaling ladders, they climbed the outer wall. The 80,000 defenders poured boiling oil down on them, loosed clouds of arrows from their chain-reinforced towers and dropped rocks.

Thousands of Crusaders died. The city held.

Francis had a different attitude about reaching Moslems for Christ. Concerning two missionary methods he wrote: "One way [to witness] is to avoid quarrels or disputes and be subject to every human creature for God's sake, so bearing witness to the fact that we are Christians. Another way is to proclaim the Word of God openly, when we see that it is God's will, calling on hearers to believe in God Almighty, Father, Son and Holy Spirit."

After the abortive attack on Demietta, Francis chose to use both ways to reach the Sultan. He boldly hiked across the desert and entered the armed camp of Melek-al-kamil. He proclaimed Christ crucified to the astonished Sultan. When Islamic scholars argued their own doctrine, Francis proposed that he and the scholar of their choosing be set on fire, the One True God would pick his own man. The scholars slipped away and the Sultan, almost persuaded, gave Francis a safe conduct back to Christian lines.

Disturbing news awaited.

The people left in charge of the Franciscan order in Italy had instituted new rules in Francis' absence. They were forbidding the Friars to eat meat—and they were allowing members to own *things!*

Francis rushed back to Portiuncula in time for the next General Meeting. He found Friars enmeshed in materialism and complaining that the simple example of Christ is too unreasonable and hard to follow.

Of course, the dissidents offered spiritualized explanations for their materialism. For instance, some wanted to own a personal Bible or prayer book.

Francis reminded them of an incident only a few years earlier when a starving woman happened on their meeting, and since they had no food on hand at that time, they sold their copy of the prayer book to feed her and conducted services from memory.

"I am your breviary; follow Christ as I do," Francis said.

Other Friars wanted books and Bibles so they could study and teach Scripture like Dominicans. That sounds reasonable, but Francis reasoned that if we Christians were to use our energy to practice the Scriptures we do understand, then we would have little energy left to scrutinize obscure verses we don't understand.

Besides, Francis recognized the snowballing aspect of materialism: He reasoned that if you own a book, you need a waterproof pouch to carry it in; then a candle to read it by and a pen to make notes with; then a desk to write on; a chair for the desk; a house for this furniture and a servant to clean the house while you study. And that servant needs . . .

"But Brother Francis," opponents argued, "Following your way we hardly have the necessities of life."

Francis said, "The foxes have dens, the birds have nests but the Son of God had nowhere to lay his head; are we better than He? Save for God, there are no such things as necessities of life."

The debate continued, and rather than see schism, Francis gave up his own most prized possession: leadership of the order he had founded.

He resigned. The Friars selected another man as leader. And Francis submitted as a common brother to him, obeying all his orders. He devoted himself to prayer, penitence and preaching to both man and beast.

In modern times much is made of Francis's exhorting birds and beasts. He's thought of as a medieval ecologist preaching to doves, flocks of sheep and at least one wolf. He did do these things, calling all nature to praise and express gratitude to the Creator. His hymn "All Creatures of Our God and King" reflects this aspect of his ministry.

Yet his ministry was primarily *for* Christ, especially as Jesus reveals himself in Matthew 25:31-45. Francis boldly tells us, "Try to realize the dignity God has conferred on you. He created and formed your body in the image of His Beloved Son, and your soul in his own likeness. Yet every creature under heaven serves, acknowledges and obeys its Creator in its own way better than you do. Even the devils were not solely responsible for crucifying him; it was you with them and you continue to crucify him by taking pleasure in your vices and sins."

The vision of Christ crucified motivated Francis's life. He thought often of the Passion and prayed, "That I may know Him, and the power of His resurrection, and the fellowship of His sufferings, being made conformable to His death."

God granted his prayer.

On September 14, 1224, as Francis prayed alone on Mount Alvernia, he saw a vision of the Savior stretched out on the hard wood of the cross, in pain yet splendid, surrounded by six dazzling wings like a seraph. When the vision passed, Francis's hands, feet and side bore excruciating wounds which bled constantly during the final two years of his life.

Francis bound rags over these stigmata to hide them. But such a thing proved difficult to conceal.

Now people sought him, no longer catcalling *Pazzo* "madman," but shouting *Il Santo* "the Saint." Unable to walk because of the crippling wounds, Francis devoted himself to prayer and hymn writing.

Although just over forty years of age, Francis contracted dropsy. As his sight failed, the personal physician of Pope Honorius treated him by cauterization.

They seared his face, chin to eyebrows, with a white-hot iron—no anesthetic.

He sang, approaching this cure.

The dropsy worsened.

Bedridden in Assisi, Francis led visiting Friars in hymns and sang ballads from his troubadour-loving days. But they had to mute their singing from the sickroom; Brother Elias, the new Minister-General of the Order, complained that "such unwonted gaiety might have an unedifying effect on devout neighbors who fear death." Elias felt that his Order's founder ought not to die like a fool but with becoming dignity.

As death approached, Francis requested that he be laid naked on the ground in a bed of ashes, his arms extended in final penitence. As a brother read St. John's account of Christ's Passion over him, Francis' last words were, "I have done my duty, may Christ now teach you yours!"

THE EXECUTIONS AT OXFORD

Thomas Cranmer (d. March 21, 1556)

*T*he cloth sacks were tied by cords so long they bumped against the loins of the two men chained to the post. A loving friend had bribed the executioner to be allowed to drape the fatal necklaces around the necks of the two Protestant bishops. The sacks were a gift of mercy; they contained gunpowder.

Light rain spattered on the bundles of kindling sticks piled over the faggots heaped at the men's feet. Crowds of curious villagers jostled for position among the students and faculty of Oxford University on this drizzly day of October 6, 1555.

Everyone strained to hear what the condemned men were saying; would they recant or would they persist in dying as heretics? A team of Roman Catholic priests urged them to turn and believe, but the two seemed more intent on talking to each other.

"Be of good heart, Brother, for God will either assuage the fury of the flame, or else strengthen us to abide it," said Nicholas Ridley, bishop of Rochester.

"Yes," agreed Hugh Latimer, bishop of Worcester. "Be of good comfort, Master Ridley, and play the man; we shall this day light such a candle, by God's grace, in England, as I trust shall never be put out."

The executioner pushed a torch into the kindling bundles and stepped back.

The fire smoldered and sputtered in the damp wood. Curls of smoke twisted upward in the wind, enveloping Latimer, but the breeze blew the heat clear of Ridley.

The crowd, knowing a contest of wills was nearing conclusion, listened intently. During his imprisonment, Latimer had said, "The highest promise that God can bring us in this life is to suffer for the truth; and one suffering for the truth turneth more than a thousand sermons."

Ridley had also spoken these confident words at his sentencing: "Although I be not of your company, yet I doubt not, but that my name is written in another place, whither this sentence will sooner send us than we should have come in the course of nature."

On the other hand, Weston, one of the judges, felt sure the heretics would recant. He told Latimer, "Your stubbornness comes of a vain glory. . . . It will do you no good when a faggot is in your beard."

And when one of the Reformers boasted, "I have the Word," Weston responded, "Yes, but we have the sword."

Now, the crowd watched to see which would hold true, the Reformers' declarations of steadfastness or Judge Weston's predictions that they would crumble.

Smoke soon suffocated Latimer; but the flame kept dying down on Ridley's side of the stake.

At first, these words of Ridley's were coherent: "O Heavenly Father, I give Thee most hearty thanks that Thou hast called me to be a professor of Thee even unto death. I beseech Thee, Lord God, have mercy upon the realm of England, and deliver her from all her enemies."

Later, he pleaded with the authorities to intercede with Queen Mary to allow his relatives to keep their property which the Crown had confiscated.

But finally, he begged the crowd, "More fire, Good People, more fire! Let the fire come up!"

In response bystanders heaped on more wood, which only smothered the blaze. A contemporary account says, "It burned all his lower parts without touching the upper. Even after his legs were consumed, spectators saw one side of his body, shirt and all, untouched by the flame."

"O Lord, have mercy upon me," he screamed as a soldier scattered the damp faggots to allow ventilation. The flame arose and Ridley actually leaned into it, bending over the chain around his waist. Flame ignited his gunpowder necklace. "His legs being wholly consumed, the upper part of his body turned over the chain and fell dead at Latimer's feet."

Neither had recanted.

Thomas Cranmer, archbishop of Canterbury, watched the burning of his two friends from the rooftop of the jail where he was confined. He had already been condemned as a Protestant and knew that he was scheduled to burn next.

As he saw Ridley, who had converted him, writhing in terrible suffering and calling, "For Christ's sake, more Fire," Cranmer probably wondered about his own grace to endure. His mind questioned,

Does God give martyrs some special ability to stand, or is pain pain whether suffered by a Christian or a godless man? Wasn't Jesus afraid of the pain of the cross when He prayed till He sweated blood in

Gethsemane? How will I hold up when my turn comes? What I believe is true, isn't it?

. . . Isn't it? What if I falter? O God, don't let me falter! But what would happen if I did? Latimer died quickly with hardly any evidence of discomfort; but Ridley stood chained with his feet in the fire for nearly an hour. . . . Which way will it be when my turn comes?

The smell of charred flesh hung in the air over Oxford. Nagging mice of doubt gnawed at Cranmer as the jailer marched him down from the rooftop.

Alone in his bleak cell, Cranmer had to settle in his own mind whether his faith, the faith of the Church of England, was eternally true or merely the whim of a lecherous king.

He remembered how he had come to the attention of Henry VIII.

Cranmer had attended Cambridge University from the time he was fourteen years old. There he distinguished himself by actually marrying "Black Joan," daughter of the tavern keeper at the Dolphin Inn. He lost his fellowship over the scandal.

Joan died in childbirth and Cranmer was reinstated and earned his doctorate in 1523. He became a lecturer at his own college.

In August 1529, people began to drop dead in the streets of Cambridge. Plague! The university closed. Students and faculty fled, hoping to escape contagion.

Cranmer and two of his students stopped at an inn, and as they drank, they engaged in a bull session ranging from campus gossip to national policy. The burning national issue of the day was "the divorce."

King Henry VIII kept a mistress, Anne Boleyn, and he wished to marry her in spite of his existing first marriage. The pope refused to allow an annulment.

In the course of tavern talk, Cranmer suggested that if the universities were to examine the situation and find that Queen

Catherine had been legally married to Henry's brother as a child, then Henry's marriage would be annulled without recourse to the pope.

Two of Henry's advisers happened to be drinking at the same tavern and overheard Cranmer's conversation. They reported to Henry, who said, "Let him be sent for out of hand. This man, I trow, has got the right sow by the ear!"

This chance encounter resulted in Cranmer's becoming one of Henry's chief advisers and eventually archbishop of Canterbury. He guided Henry through his next five stormy marriages and led the English Reformation after Henry's break from Rome.

Cranmer played a vital part in the translation of the English Bible. Opponents of the Bible in the vernacular attempted to delay the translation in committee. Cranmer, in complaining about this tactic and referring to various private translations on the market, wrote, "The same [private copies] may be sold and read of every person . . . until such time that we, the bishops, shall set forth a better translation, which I think will not be till a day after doomsday."

He expedited the work, and soon Cranmer's Bible, an immediate forerunner of the Authorized (King James) Version, was chained to a pillar in every church, available to any reader.

To most Reformers—whose beliefs ranged from Zwingli's view that the sacrament is purely a commemorative ordinance to Luther's view of consubstantiation—worship of the communion bread represented idolatry.

Feelings ran high on the subject.

Cranmer renounced the mass saying, "As the devil was a liar at the beginning and the father of lies—this Infernal Spirit is now endeavoring to restore the Latin satisfactory masses, a thing of his invention and devise . . . a plain contradiction to antiquity and Inspired Writing and is besides replete with many horrible blasphemies."

He added, "As our Regeneration in Christ by Baptism is spiritual, even so our eating and drinking is a spiritual feeding, which kind of regeneration and feeding requireth no real and corporeal Presence of Christ, but only His Presence in spirit, in grace and effectual operation."

Because Cranmer, Ridley and Latimer held such views, they discouraged the use of an altar in the English churches and initiated the use of a communion table. This was a major factor in their heresy trials.

The idea that a person could choose his own theological views, even if those views were wrong, had not gained wide acceptance in the 1500s. Even Reformers such as John Knox argued, "It is not only lawful to punish to the death such as labor to subvert the true religion, but magistrates and people are *bound* to do so."

Therefore, Cranmer and his friends, when in power, had been involved in burning at the stake people they considered heretics. At times, in his official capacity, Cranmer found himself condemning to death people who publicly proclaimed the same views he held privately.

The Reformation followed a course of gains and losses through the reigns of King Henry VIII and Edward VI; then Queen Mary—Bloody Mary—ascended through political turmoil to the throne.

She remained a devout Catholic.

"I set more by the salvation of one soul than by ten kingdoms," she said.

She set out to gain the salvation of English souls.

Cranmer, Ridley and Latimer had backed an abortive maneuver to place a Protestant, Lady Jane Grey, on the throne. Mary's ascension assured their arrest. Hundreds of Protestant pastors and leaders fled to the Continent, but these three chose to remain in England.

Mary intended to restore the old religion gradually, reasonably. However, zealous Protestants antagonized her. Some shaved the head of a dead dog so it resembled a priest's tonsure and flung the putrid beast into a council meeting she attended. Some disrupted masses, stoned priests and desecrated Catholic altars. Someone even broke into the queen's bedchamber and plastered the walls with violent anti-Catholic posters which made sick, dirty jokes about Mary's inability to get pregnant.

Mary reacted. She instructed, "I believe it would be well to inflict punishment at the beginning, without much cruelty or passion, but without however omitting to do such justice on those who chose by their false doctrines to deceive simple persons . . . and above all, I wish no one to be burned in London . . . and that during such executions . . . some good and pious sermons be preached."

The queen saw nothing ironic about pious sermons at a public burning; and she saw nothing cruel about burning heretics who might lead her subjects astray. According to her, burning Protestants was a pious act which ought to edify the onlookers.

Following the queen's instruction, guards removed Cranmer, Ridley and Latimer to Oxford University. A lengthy trial before the top scholars of the country ensued. The trio had to defend each point of their beliefs, calling on Scripture, history, church fathers and religious precedents.

Political, religious and personal enemies they had made during their years in power now determined to publicly humiliate them.

Usually Ridley defended himself eloquently, but one day when he desired to "speak my forty words" (a 16th-century idiom meaning "to have my say") the judge gave him the chance to talk. But when he started his defense, the audience began to chant "ONE—TWO—THREE . . ." They shouted him down when he reached precisely forty words.

After the deaths of Ridley and Latimer, the court continued toying with Cranmer, alternating harsh treatment with privileges.

On February 14, 1556, his tormentors made him appear in Christ's Church, Oxford, wearing the full regalia and vestments of archbishop: alb, rochet, cope, miter, ring, rozier and pallium. Methodically, they snatched away each item chanting, "This is the man that has pulled down churches. . . . This is the man that deprived the Pope. . . . This is the man that . . ."

They shaved off his hair and scraped his fingernails and toenails which had been anointed with holy oil at his consecration. They returned him to his dark cell to think.

A few days later, they allowed him to bathe, and they moved him to the Oxford Deanery. There he was treated with dignity as he dined with the faculty, browsed in the library, bowled or played chess with his intellectual peers. Then abruptly, back to the filthy cell.

News came. The queen wanted Cranmer as her officer, the messenger joyfully reported—if she could have Cranmer the Catholic.

I, THOMAS CRANMER, late Archbishop of Canterbury, renounce, abhor, and detest all manner of heresies and errors. . . . I confess One, Holy and Catholic Church visible, without which there can be no salvation, and, thereof I acknowledge the Bishop of Rome to be the supreme Head on earth . . . Pope and Christ's vicar unto whom all Christian people ought to be subject.

In the space of a few days, Cranmer penned six similar documents.

His enemies determined to burn him anyhow.

In keeping with the queen's desire for pious sermons at an

execution, a service was set for March 21, 1556. Rain forced the service to be held inside. The high point of the proceedings was for the condemned archbishop to repeat his recantation and to publicly confess his sin of heresy.

A huge crowd gathered.

In a letter written two days later, a Catholic eyewitness describes what happened when Cranmer prayed:

"O God, Thou wast not made man . . . for few or small offenses. Nor didst Thou give Thy Son unto death . . . for our little and small sins only, but for all the greatest sins . . . O Lord, Whose property is always to have mercy. . . . Now I come to the Great Thing that troubleth my conscience more than any other thing that ever I said or did in my life; and that is the setting abroad of writings contrary to the truth . . . writ for fear of death and to save my life. . . .

"And forasmuch as my hand offended in writing contrary to my heart, Therefore my hand shall first be punished . . . it shall be first burned. . . ."

Here he was suffered to speak no more. Then he was carried away and a great number . . . ran after him, exhorting him. . . .

At the stake he professed that he died in all such opinions as he had taught, and oft repented him of his recantation.

"This is the hand that wrote it [he said] and therefore shall it suffer first. . . ."

Fire being now put to him, he stretched out his right hand and thrust it into the flame, and held it there a good space, before the fire came to any other part of his body, where his hand was seen of every man sensibly burning, crying out with a loud voice, 'This hand hath offended.' As soon as the fire was got up, he was very soon dead, never stirring or crying all the while.

Thus, like an arrow which wobbles in its flight yet strikes the target center, Thomas Cranmer ended his career. It took the fiery stake to teach him the truth of his own words when he said:

> I have learned from experience . . . that God never shines forth more brightly, and puts out the beams of His mercy and consolation, or of strength and firmness of spirit, more clearly or impressively upon the minds of his people, than when they are under the most extreme pain and distress, both of mind and body, that He may then more especially show Himself to the God of His people, when He seems to have altogether forsaken them; then glorifying them when He is thought to be destroying them. So that we may say with Paul, "When I am weak, then I am strong."

A Mystic
Lady

Jeanne Marie Guyon (d. June 9, 1717)

In his palace at Versailles, Louis XIV, king of France and all her dominions by the grace of God, regularly entertained as many as 10,000 dukes and duchesses, counts and countesses, marquises and marchionesses, bishops, priests, monks, abbots, soldiers, courtesans, ambassadors, guests—and their servants, who each ranked above or below other servants according to the positions of the employer.

Every one of these people wanted something from the king. And whatever each one wanted had to be gained at the expense of someone else.

The king played all these people off against each other in ploys of elaborately organized chaos. He passionately believed in the divine right of kings and felt that, as God's appointed ruler, all persons and property in France belonged to him to dispose of as he pleased.

The king also believed that the moral laws incumbent on ordinary men did not bind him. This belief often expressed itself in licentious sexual behavior. The king felt any husband ought to feel proud if his wife or daughter had been of service to the monarch.

The extent to which a woman pleased or failed to please the taste of the king often determined the position, wealth and position of herself and her family. Once, when a girl who sold chickens caught the king's fancy, she moved to the head of the line while duchesses and countesses seethed.

Men achieved rank for no more noble reasons. Public officials, nobles, army generals—even pastors, bishops and archbishops—were appointed or removed at the whim of the king.

A daring handful of Christians lived in this decadent atmosphere. Their lives cut through the elaborate rituals of the court and rebuked its vanity. And most noteworthy among these people was Madame Jeanne Marie Guyon.

The queen of England had been a guest at the estate of Jeanne Marie's father when Madame Guyon was a little girl. The queen was so taken with the child's beauty that she wanted her as a maiden in the English court; but the father, Seigneur de la Mothe Vergonville, a lord and a millionaire, kept his daughter for France.

The little girl spent most of her youth in various convents being raised and educated by nuns. When she was age sixteen, her father arranged a marriage for her with the thirty-eight-year-old M. Jacques Guyon, a high-ranking nobleman with vast wealth.

The couple lived in one of M. Guyon's townhouses in Paris, where they enjoyed the glitter and glamour of the city and the court. She gave birth to several healthy children.

Yet, although she was noted for her beauty and had wealth, position, estates, carriages, gowns, children and a husband who loved her; and although she had been raised in a religious atmosphere and was sensitive to spiritual things and supported numerous charities—even with all that, the young woman still felt a deep hunger, a yearning, a longing for something more. Something vital was missing from her life.

A visiting Franciscan brother told her, "Your efforts have been unsuccessful, Madame, because you have sought without what you can only find within. Accustom yourself to seek God in your heart, and you will not fail to find Him."

This evaluation haunted her.

In her autobiography, she says:

Having said these words, the Franciscan left me. They were to me like the stroke of a dart which pierced my heart asunder. I felt at this instant deeply wounded with the love of God—a wound so delightful that I desired it never might be healed. These words brought into my heart what I had been seeking so many years. . . . Oh infinite Goodness! Thou wast so near, and I ran hither and thither seeking Thee and yet found Thee not. . . .

I was poor in the midst of riches, and ready to perish with hunger near a table plentifully spread and a continual feast. Oh, Beauty, ancient and new! Why have I known Thee so late? Alas, I sought Thee where Thou wast not, and did not seek Thee where Thou wast. . . .

My heart was quite changed, that God was there; for from that moment, He had given me an experience of His presence in my soul—not merely as an object intellectually perceived, but as a thing really possessed after the sweetest manner. . . .

I slept not at all that night, because Thy love, O my God, flowed in me like delicious oil, and burned as a fire which

was going to destroy all that was left of self in an instant.
Words and sentiments such as these fill her 500-page autobiography. The passage you have just read is typical of her writing
in joyous passion for Christ.

Although she was only twenty years old when she discovered
Christ in her heart, these words characterize the overall tone
of her life from that point on with little fluctuation.

A burning, almost mystical awareness of the love of Christ
permeates all that she experienced. In court, in the business
world, in prison, in church, the love of Christ preoccupied Madame Guyon, whatever else might be happening around her.

She devoted herself to intense prayers of adoration and to
charitable works: founding hospitals, giving scholarships, building churches, funding monasteries and convents, caring for
individual poor families. Her giving to the poor became so
extensive that she had to hire a steward to disperse gifts anon-
ymously. But at the same time she was not above washing the
infected sores of poor strangers or the wounds of soldiers with
her own hands.

Her parents died, leaving her a title and a fortune of her
own. Two of her children also died. Then, in 1676, her husband died after a lengthy illness, leaving the twenty-eight-year-
old widow with incredible wealth and vast estates to manage.

Marriage proposals poured in; she refused them all. For a
time she considered becoming a nun, entering a convent, or
going to China as a missionary, but she realized that huge
numbers of people depended on her for their employment on
her various estates for their only income to support their families. She felt that managing these estates was a God-appointed
responsibility.

Among the problems her husband left when he died was a
decision on a complicated lawsuit which involved twenty-two
different claimants and their lawyers trying to divide income

from one estate. They all had appealed to him for judgment, and the urgent need for a decision about the settlement fell on the young widow's shoulders.

She prayed for divine guidance in the complex matter and settled it to the satisfaction of all parties within a month!

She said, "They accepted it and signed it. I afterwards learned that they were so well pleased with what I had done, that they not only commended it much, but published it abroad everywhere. The hand of the Lord was in it. It was God who gave me wisdom."

While noted for her business acumen on one level, Madame Guyon's prayers led her into states of religious rapture on another. These two elements combine in a contract which she renewed yearly on the anniversary of her religious conversion:

I henceforth take Jesus Christ to be mine. I promise to receive Him as a husband to me. And I give myself to Him, unworthy though I am, to be His spouse. I ask of Him, in this marriage of spirit with spirit, that I may be of the same mind with Him—meek, pure, nothing in myself, and united in God's will. And, pledged as I am to be His, I accept, as part of my marriage portion, the temptations and sorrows, the crosses and the contempt which fell to Him.—Jeanne M. B. de la Mothe Guyon, Sealed with her ring.

Madame Guyon became noted as a leading figure in a Christian movement called Quietism. Essentially, she recognized that God is all; nothing else counts. She felt so identified with his will and his love that no lesser thing deserved her attention. A person in love thinks about the beloved all the time, no matter what else is going on.

Now for an extreme example.

Once, when traveling with a party of other lords and ladies by carriage near a flooding river, the bank caved in, sweeping the road away. The carriage overturned in the flood and began sinking. Drowning horses screamed, kicking and struggling in the water. Footmen, coachmen, lords and ladies scrambled for safety.

Madame Guyon said, "Others threw themselves out of the carriage in excessive fright. But I found my thoughts so much taken up with God, that I had no distinct sense of the danger to which we were really exposed. God, to whom my mind was inwardly drawn, delivered me from the perils to which we were exposed, with scarcely a thought on my part of avoiding them. . . . In this state of mind, I can not fail to be content in the trials which He sees fit to send upon me."

Would Almighty God get upset and panic over a minor incident like a traffic accident, she reasoned? No. Then why should a person attuned to his mind and will be concerned? She had something more important to think about than a carriage accident: her adoration of the Living Christ.

She enjoyed God so much that she attempted to stifle her own will and live totally in accord with his. When two well-tuned lutes are in perfect concert, strum one and the other also vibrates with sound even though it has not been touched. That is how she explained her feelings about God's will.

She said, "There is the same spirit in both, the same sound, one pure harmony. It was thus that my will seemed to be in harmony with God's will. . . .

"The soul must submit itself to be conducted, from moment to moment, by the Divine hand; and to be annihilated, as it were, by the strokes of His providence without complaining, or desiring anything beside what it now has."

But unfortunately, she said, we wish to direct God instead of resigning ourselves to be directed by him. We wish to take the lead, and to follow in a way of our own selection instead of submissively following where God sees fit to conduct us. Therefore, many who are called to the enjoyment of God himself and not merely to the gifts of God, spend all their lives in pursuing and in feeding on "little consolations," she said.

In July 1681, she and her maid, who was her best friend and a like-minded Quietist, took her five-year-old daughter and left Paris for a missionary trip near the Protestant stronghold of Geneva. King Louis XIV had sent troops into the area to kill or convert the heretics. Madame Guyon felt that Protestants and Catholics alike devoted too much energy to observing hollow forms of religion while neglecting internal purity and truth.

As part of her mission, she endowed convents, established schools, founded hospitals and helped serve in soup kitchens. But by far the most impact from her missionary work came from her personal witnessing.

As a rule when she moved into a city, she rented a modest cottage and retired inside to devote herself to prayer. She described one of her stops at the town of Thonon:

It had the look of the greatest poverty and had no chimney except in the kitchen through which one was obliged to pass to go to the chamber. I gave up the largest chamber to my daughter and maid. The chamber reserved to my self was a very small one and I ascended to it by a ladder. Having no furniture of my own except some beds, quite plain and homely, I bought a few cheap chairs and such articles of earthen or wooden ware as were necessary. Never did I enjoy a greater content than in this hovel. It seemed to me entirely comfortable to the littleness and simplicity which characterize the true life in Christ.

Madame Guyon made no announcement of her presence in town, but within days a steady stream of people began to call at her door seeking spiritual help. Milkmaids and knights, bishops and drunks, streetwalkers and nuns, monks and merchants all felt strangely moved to seek the prayers and counsel of this quiet woman who kept to her own house praying. Lines formed at dawn and the last visitor seldom left before midnight. Some turned to Christ; some left the house to throw rocks through her windows. She prayed with all.

She said, "People flocked together from all sides, far and near. Friars, priests, men of the world, maids, wives, widows, all came, one after another to hear. . . . Many were the souls which submitted to God at this time."

Some priests, she said, "were grievously chagrined that a woman should be so much flocked to and sought after. For, looking at the things as they were in themselves, and not as they were in God, who uses what instrument He pleases, they forgot, in their contempt for the instrument, to admire the goodness and grace manifested through it."

During the years of her missionary trip, she also wrote several books, including a twenty-volume commentary on the Bible and *A Short Method of Prayer*. Her book on prayer emphasized the importance of the internal spiritual life over mere external forms of religion.

She said:

It is not actions in themselves considered which please Him, but the inward spirit with which they are done; and especially the constant ready obedience to every discovery of His will, even in the minutest things.

It was my object to instruct them [people who came to her for counsel] in the way of living by simple faith. I remarked to them that the way of living by faith was much more glorious to God and much more advantageous to the soul than any other method of living.

This stand on faith got her into serious trouble.

Persecutions abounded. People burned her books. Some called her insane. Some said she was a witch. Some loved her. Some hated her. They praised or condemned.

She ignored them all equally as she sailed serenely on, following what she believed to be God's will. God's will led her to return to Paris.

Trouble for Madame Guyon appeared to come from several sources—yet, she said it only came from one source.

The several sources included relatives who hoped to eliminate her so they could control the Guyon fortune. Her purity of life offended some of the ladies of the court who saw her simple lifestyle and piety as a rebuke to their own licentiousness. Protestants viewed her missionary efforts as a papist plot. Some Catholic archbishops said she was a living saint while others condemned her as a heretic. King Louis XIV wanted Madame Guyon to give her daughter, now age twelve, in marriage to a notorious old rake to whom the king owed money; the girl's estate would pay off the king's debt.

Madame Guyon would not consent to the marriage. She was arrested and locked in prison. The king signed the *lettre de cachet* on January 29, 1688.

She said, "Amid the various trials and temptations to which I was exposed, I bore everything with the greatest tranquility, without taking any care to justify or defend myself. Having faith in God, I left it with Him to order everything as He should see best in regard to me."

The reason she could enjoy tranquility and concentrate on her devotions even while separated from her daughter, her wealth and her freedom was that she believed all the trouble came from only one single source—the love of God.

She said of her persecutors:

They only did what God permitted them to do, which enabled me always to keep God in sight. . . . When we suffer, we should always remember that God inflicts the blow. Wicked men, it is true, are not infrequently His instruments; and the fact does not diminish, but simply develops their wickedness. But when we are so mentally disposed that we love the strokes we suffer, regarding them as coming from God, and as expressions of what He sees best for us, we are then in the proper state to look forgivingly and kindly upon the subordinate instrument which He permits to smite us.

Not only did she see God as the source of every Christian's trouble, she also saw him as the source of every comfort. When she fell gravely ill in prison, to the point of dying, her jailers—against the king's express orders—called in a physician, an action she saw as another evidence of God's love.

She said, "It was God who put it into their hearts and gave them the determination to do it. . . . After bringing me down, He was pleased to raise me up again."

The king promised to release her from prison within eight days if she would consent to her daughter's marriage to his crony. She again refused.

She replied, "God allows suffering, but never allows wrong. I see clearly that it is His will that I should remain in prison and endure the pains which are connected with it; and I am entirely content that it should be so. I can never buy my liberty at the expense of sacrificing my daughter."

It looked then as though she would stay locked up for the rest of her life. Louis XIV did not take kindly to anyone, even members of the highest aristocracy, who opposed his will.

Whatever the pampered king intended, God must have wanted Madame Guyon to get out of jail free.

It happened like this.

Madame Guyon's case had become somewhat of a novelty; seeing a highborn lady, a millionaire heiress, in jail became a spectator sport for members of the court. Lords and ladies flocked to see her in jail, and lines of noble gawkers filed past her cell.

One of these tourists was Madame Françoise de Maintenon. This young woman knew the ropes at court. The king kept a series of mistresses with whom he fathered numerous children. The mistresses played fun and games, but someone had to watch the children. One of the mistresses hired Françoise as governess for the king's unofficial brood. From that position, she undermined the children's mothers and moved into the king's bedroom herself. There she eliminated the competition.

The king doted on her.

But, when Madame de Maintenon saw Madame Guyon in prison, something about the prisoner attracted the courtesan. The godly woman appeared to have an inner peace, an indefinable Something which was missing from the whirl of court parties, affairs and intrigues.

Writing to a friend, the king's favorite mistress said, "I have been young and beautiful, have had a high relish of pleasure, and been the universal object of love. . . . I have at last risen to favor; but I protest to you, my dear, that every one of these conditions leaves in the mind a dismal vacuity."

The mistress determined to free the prisoner. She explained the law of supply and demand to the raunchy king, and he promptly released Madame Guyon.

The younger woman invited Madame Guyon to live with her in the palace the king supplied for his favorites. There Madame Guyon conducted home prayer meetings and counseling sessions for the young ladies of the king's court!

Palace or prison made no difference to Madame Guyon, so absorbed was she in the love of Christ.

She said:

I live, therefore, as well as I can express it, out of myself and all other creatures, in union with God. It is thus that God, by His sanctifying grace, has become to me All in all. . . . I find God in everything which is, and in everything which comes to pass. The creature is nothing. God is ALL. . . .

Viewed in relation to the creature, everything is dark—viewed in relation to God, everything is light.

All that I know is that God is infinitely holy, righteous and happy; that all goodness is in Him; and that, as to myself, I am a mere nothing.

For these sentiments her enemies accused her of being a pantheist. They subjected her books, her letters, her life to close scrutinizing by committee after committee. Eventually, even Madame Maintenon's heart apparently changed, and she too joined the ranks of Madame Guyon's enemies.

Having lost the protection of the king's favorite mistress, Madame Guyon was arrested again, this time for heresy, and locked in the Bastille. The famous Man in the Iron Mask, thought by many to be the king's twin brother, was confined in the Bastille at the same time she was there. The Bastille held the reputation of being the most horrible prison on earth.

There Madame Guyon spent four years in solitary confinement.

She prayed, "I, being in the Bastille, said to Thee, Oh my God, If Thou art pleased to render me a spectacle to men and angels, Thy holy will be done! All I ask is that Thou wilt be with and save those who love Thee."

As a condition of her release when she finally got out, the king forced her to sign a written vow swearing that she would never reveal what had happened to her inside the awful dungeons.

After she died in 1717 at the age of 69, her family found among her papers a poem she had written about being in prison, but even that poem about confinement in the Bastille does not break the vow she had made.

Here is what she wrote:

A little bird I am,

Shut from the fields of air;
And in my cage I sit and sing
To Him who placed me there;
Well pleased a prisoner to be,
Because, my God, it pleased Thee.

My cage confines me round;
Abroad I cannot fly;
But though my wing is closely bound,
My heart's at liberty.
My prison walls can not control
The flight, the freedom of my soul.

Oh, it is good to soar
These bolts and bars above,
To Him whose purpose I adore,
Whose providence I love;
And in Thy mighty will to find
The joy, the freedom of the mind.

The Best Preparation

Susannah Wesley (d. July 23, 1742)

The maid brought the baby to the new mother's room for it to nurse. But when Susannah Wesley, only half-awake, nestled her child to her breast, she found it was dead.

"She composed herself as well as she could, and that day got it buried," her husband wrote.

Such tragedies haunted Susannah Wesley.

Ten of her nineteen children died before they were two years old; five in the space of four years. And one of her daughters was deformed.

But her faith in God sustained her. An entry in her diary reads, "All my sufferings, by the admirable management of Omnipotent Goodness, have concurred to promote my spiritual and eternal good. Glory be to Thee, O Lord."

Susannah was the mother of John Wesley, founder of Methodism, and of Charles Wesley, who wrote over a thousand hymns such as "Hark, the Herald Angels Sing" and "Christ the Lord Is Risen Today."

Although she is best known for her sons, family letters and those portions of her diary which remain show that she was a spiritual giant in her own right.

Surviving records show that Susannah was the youngest of twenty-five children born to a Nonconformist English clergyman, the Reverend Samuel Annesley.

The Anglican church was the official state religion of England. Anyone who worshiped in a different mode was termed a Nonconformist or Dissenter.

An internal and external spiritual battle over the question of whether or not to conform colored Susannah's whole life.

When she was a girl, the government passed the Act of Uniformity of 1662. This law required every clergyman to declare his "unfeigned assent to all and everything contained and prescribed in the Book of Common Prayer."

The day that the law went into effect, thousands of dissenting pastors, including Susannah's father, were forced to leave their churches—and their parsonages. They were forbidden by law to live within five miles of any place they had ever preached. They were also forbidden to teach in any school, public or private.

Anyone who even allowed a dissenting minister or his family in his home was fined, transported to a colony or imprisoned. Over 5,000 Nonconformists reportedly died in English prisons for their faith. Is it any wonder that bitter feelings developed between the factions.

Yet, although her family suffered for their Nonconformist faith, as a teen-ager Susannah came to believe that God appoints earthly governments and that obeying him requires his people to obey the laws of the land. She joined the established church.

Susannah wrote, "Before I was full 13, I had drawn up an account of the whole transaction under the which I had included the main of the controversy between them [the dissenters] and the Established Church, as far as it had come to my knowledge."

Thus, she re-evaluated her father's religion and influenced her fiance, Samuel Wesley, whom she married when she was nineteen and he twenty-six, to worship with the established Church of England. Samuel abandoned his Nonconformist faith to become an Anglican priest.

Two years after their marriage Susannah bore her first child. She gave birth to eighteen other children—delivered by a midwife without anesthesia or antiseptic, born in the space of twenty-one years.

Her husband became an Anglican clergyman and a writer, but not a successful one. He wrote a 9,000-line metrical poem on the life of Christ and spent years writing a dissertation on the book of Job. Only 500 copies of his Job work were printed, and not all of those sold.

He was appointed to a parish where many Nonconformist families lived, and tensions grew between the pastor and some members of his reluctant congregation.

Many nights, mobs surrounded the Wesley parsonage, beating drums, firing guns in the air and pelting the house with stones. The local congregation refused to pay his salary.

He tried to farm his land to add to the family income, but his barns mysteriously caught fire and his venture failed.

Members of his own congregation had him arrested and sent to debtor's prison, leaving Susannah and the children with only thirty shillings.

He was probably referring to the mob attacks on his home

when he said it, but any father of nineteen children might well identify with what Samuel confided in a friend: "Jail is a paradise in comparison of the life I led before I came hither," he said.

At home with the children, Susannah did not fare so well. For one thing, the mob attacks did not stop, even though the pastor was in prison. For another, Susannah endured terrible poverty.

Yet she survived.

She said, "I never did want for bread. But then, I had so much care to get it before it was eaten, and to pay for it after, it has often made it very unpleasant to me. And I think to have bread on such terms is the next degree of wretchedness to having none at all."

Now in those days, food was not provided to prisoners by the state; if they were to eat, it was up to their families to provide food at the jail. Susannah proposed to her husband that she sell her wedding ring in order to buy his food while he was in jail; but he preferred to go hungry rather than have Susannah sell her only earthly treasure.

While she was waiting for her husband's release, a vandal set fire to her garden and slashed the udders of the family's cows. She had to scrounge for milk as well as bread.

"The best preparation I know of for suffering is a regular and exact performance of present duty," she said.

Faith and discipline motivated her life.

She said, "Religion is nothing else than doing the will of God and not our own. Heaven or Hell depends on this alone."

Her steadfast prayer life was her outstanding characteristic. No matter what might intervene, when the clock struck certain hours, she retired to her room for prayer.

One legend concerning this remarkable woman tells that when the children got exasperating, Susannah would toss the hem of her long white apron over her head to hide her face for prayer. When they saw Mother with her apron up, the children walked softly.

She taught her children in a household school six hours each day. On each child's fifth birthday, he or she had to learn the alphabet.

She gave each child one hour alone with her undivided attention each week.

She was loving but strict, aiming to "break the child's will, but not its spirit."

She said:

In order to form the minds of children, the first thing to be done is to conquer their will and bring them to an obedient temper. Proceed by slow degrees as they are able to bear it.

I call cruel parents who permit their children to get habits which they know must be afterwards broken.

As self-will is the root of all sin and misery, so whatever cherishes this in children ensures their after wretchedness.

Our children were quickly made to understand they might have nothing they cried for and instructed to speak handsomely for what they wanted.

Susannah recognized that her child-rearing methods were unusual even in the light of eighteenth-century ideas of strictness. And she knew that most parents would not expend as much effort as she did; but she regarded her home as her God-ordained place of ministry.

She said, "There are few, if any, who would devote about twenty years of the prime of life in hopes to save the souls of their children."

Her personal devotions made her aware of Christ in all areas of her life. "Grant me grace, O Lord, to be wholly a Christian" was her frequent prayer.

A letter to her son Samuel advises, "Endeavor to act upon principle and do not live like the rest of mankind, who pass through the world like straws upon a river, which are carried which way the stream or wind drive them.

"Get as deep an impression on your mind as is possible of the constant presence of the Great and Holy God. He is about our beds and about our paths and spies out all our ways."

When referring to her husband, Susannah used the words "My Master," but she also once said, "My own experience hath since convinced me that he is one of those who, our Saviour saith, are not so wise in their generation as the children of this world!"

She once wrote to John Wesley, " 'Tis a misfortune peculiar to our family that your father and I seldom think alike."

You see, at some point in her adult faith development, Susannah began to be more inclined toward the nonconformity of her girlhood again. Again she appears to have struggled with internal questions about God-ordained authority and personal conscience.

After Samuel got out of prison, this internal struggle of faith placed odd stresses on her marriage to a man she herself had thoroughly convinced to conform to the Anglican mode of worship.

Prayer did not unite the Wesleys. In fact, they once even separated over the issue of what to pray for.

When she refused to say "Amen" to her husband's prayer for King William, whom she did not feel was the rightful king, her husband left her. She still refused to say "Amen," but the next year the king fell, broke his neck and died. The stiff-necked Wesleys reunited without either one losing face.

Samuel Wesley ardently supported England's war with Spain. Susannah Wesley did not.

While Samuel was in London working for the war effort, he wanted her to pray for victory.

Her letter to him said, "Since I am not satisfied of the lawfulness of the war, I cannot beg a blessing on our arms, nor pray for the good success of those arms which were taken up, I think, unlawfully."

And, during the winter of 1712, when she, a mere woman, contrary to what he felt were biblical injunctions, preached to fifty people in her barn during a Sunday home-prayer meeting, while he, God's ordained clergyman for the parish, was away on business.

Well, to say the least, he was unhappy.

So was she.

His authoritarian rebuke brought out the Dissenter in her and she wrote:

And where is the harm in this? If I and my children went visiting on Sunday nights, or if we admitted of impertinent visits, as too many do who think themselves good Christians, perhaps it would be thought no scandalous practice, though in truth it would be so. Therefore, why any should reflect upon you, let your station be what it will, because your wife endeavors to draw people to the church, and to restrain them by reading and other persuasions from their profanation of God's most holy day, I cannot conceive. . . . For my part, I value no censure on this account!

Yet, even with their differences, Samuel and Susannah loved each other.

She wrote her brother in India, "He is not fit for worldly business, but where he lives I will live, and where he dies, I will die and there will I be buried."

And a poem Samuel wrote about her contains these lines:

She graced my humble roof, and blessed my life,

Blessed me by a far greater name than wife.

One day, the humble roof she graced caught fire, ignited by irate parishioners on February 9, 1709.

All of the family escaped but six-year-old John. He clung to a window frame, afraid to jump. A neighbor stood on Samuel's shoulders to reach the boy. The flaming roof caved in just as John was rescued.

All of the family's possessions that remained after the fire were a hymn sheet and a page from the family Bible which said, "Sell all thou hast. Take up thy cross, and follow me."

"I do intend to be more particularly careful of the soul of this child," she wrote in her journal on the day of the fire.

As John Wesley grew up, his mother used his being "plucked as a brand from the burning" to remind him that God saved him for some great work.

She did this as long as she lived. When he went to college, she wrote, "I was glad to hear you got safe to Oxford, and would have told you sooner had I been at liberty from pain of body and other severer trials not convenient to mention. . . . Our nature is frail; our passions strong; our wills biased; and our security, generally speaking, consists much more certainly in avoiding great temptations than in conquering them."

Now Samuel Wesley had served his tense parish for thirty-nine years and eventually died at his post, leaving Susannah an impoverished widow, dependent on her grown children for her daily bread. The church turned her out of the parsonage.

She had to travel from house to house, living with first this child then that one for a few months at a time. By this time all twenty-five of her brothers and sisters had died, and she had also lost eleven of her children.

Her faith remained viable, even joyous, in this sad situation.

She wrote, "Though man is born to trouble, yet I believe there is scarce a man to be found upon earth but, take the whole course of his life, hath more mercies than afflictions, and much more pleasure than pain. I am sure it has been so in my case."

More trials awaited her.

God called her two youngest sons, John and Charles, to leave England as established church missionaries to the Indians in the American colony of Georgia. If they went away, who would support her? After all, most of her other sons were already dead.

Her faith in God's providence answered this challenge to her old-age security.

Follow Christ, she told her sons. Leave me and go to Georgia. Be missionaries with my blessing.

"Had I twenty sons I should rejoice that they were all so employed, though I should never see them again," she said.

She saw John and Charles again all too soon. Their mission failed miserably, and they came back to England in defeat.

Now, she had been married to an Anglican clergyman for most of her life, and her sons had followed their father's example and had taken holy orders in the church which had persecuted her dissenting father; but, not long after their return in disgrace from America, both her sons underwent dynamic spiritual experiences. And though they never separated from the established church, they began to exhibit some very non-conforming religious practices.

Their enthusiasm for Christ and their zeal for souls made many of their fellow Anglican clergymen uncomfortable, and John Wesley was barred from preaching from most church pulpits.

He began the virtually unheard-of practice of preaching to crowds in the open air. Often, his aged mother stood right there beside him while he preached.

When he went back to his father's former parish, now the people had turned conservative! The pastor refused to let him preach in the church, so John Wesley walked outside into the church graveyard and climbed on top of his father's tombstone to preach to the huge crowd which had gathered to hear him.

As Susannah grew older and more feeble, John fixed up a room for her in an abandoned cannon factory, the foundry building which he had converted into headquarters for the Methodists, and there she died on July 23, 1742.

Were her struggles of faith, both internal and external, worth the suffering she endured?

In her latter years she said, "And these very sufferings have, by the blessing of God, been of excellent use, and proved the most proper means of reclaiming me from a vain conversation [lifestyle]; insomuch that I cannot say I had better have been without this affliction, this disease, this loss, want, contempt or reproach.

"All my sufferings . . . have concurred to promote my spiritual and eternal good. . . . Glory be to Thee, O Lord!"

WIDOWS OUGHT NOT TO BURN

William Carey (d. June 9, 1834)

*F*irst, the girl donned her most sumptuous silk gowns and bedecked herself with her finest jewelry. Then, her attendants poured pitchers of melted butter over her, soaking her completely.

Six times she circled the pile of wood on the river bank, tossing sweetmeats to the cheering crowd. She climbed the wooden stack and laid down by the dead man. She put one arm under the corpse's neck, the other over it.

The attendants heaped dried cocoa leaves on top of the pair and poured on more melted butter. Two stout men stretched a long bamboo pole over her and her dead husband and pushed down on each end. Other attendants began soaking these two guards with water so they could stand the heat when fire was put to the pile.

As soon as the fire was kindled, the people watching began to chant, "Hare Krishna. Hare Krishna."

"It was impossible to have heard the woman had she groaned, or even cried aloud, on account of the mad noise of the people, and it was impossible for her to stir or struggle on account of the bamboos, which were held down on her like the levers of a press," wrote William Carey, missionary to India, after he witnessed this Suttee, the burning of a widow on her husband's funeral pyre.

Indian marriage customs often linked elderly men with girls barely into puberty; for twelve-year-old widows to be burned was not uncommon.

When Carey tried to intervene: "They told me it was a great act of holiness, and added in a surly manner that if I did not like to see it I might go further off. . . . I told them that I would not go, that I was determined to stay and see the murder, and that I should certainly bear witness of it at the tribunal of God."

Carey attempted to stop this practice by influencing the British governor of India, Lord Amherst. But the governor later wrote, "While the diminution of the rite was desirable, to prohibit it entirely was inexpedient at the time."

An 1808 article in the *Edinburgh Review* summed up the official attitude toward missionary endeavor in India: "It is true the Hindus drown themselves in the Ganges, torture themselves in various ways, and burn their widows; but then it must be considered that they do this willingly and in the cheerful performance of religious duties."

The profitable East India Company, which held a virtual monopoly on all trade between England and the Orient, did not countenance missionaries disrupting the sincere religious practices of the natives under their control. A spokesman in the British Parliament denounced Carey and his fellow missionaries as "apostates from the loom and anvil, and renegades from the lowest handicraft employments."

In a way, his evaluation was correct.

William Carey had begun his career as an apprentice shoemaker in Hackleton, England, where he got into serious trouble.

The young apprentice was supposed to collect some outstanding accounts owed to his master. At the same time he collected tips as his own due. When a customer gave him a counterfeit shilling for himself, apparently as a souvenir lucky coin, Carey exchanged it for good money belonging to his master and tried to pass it off as real money.

When he saw his master and the customer talking, he feared that his deed would be discovered, for at the time theft of a shilling or more called for the death penalty. He prayed that God would get him through this problem, but, as he later wrote, "A gracious God did not get me safely through."

He was unveiled as an embezzler, and although he was not prosecuted, the shame of being unmistakably labeled as a sinful cheat caused him to turn to Christ.

The shoemaker's conversion grew evident in his work. When someone suggested some money-saving shortcuts for production, he responded, "I can not do that; I must make each pair of shoes as though Christ himself would wear them."

One day Carey found a book printed in odd letters. The strange characters enchanted him. When someone told him the language was Greek, he began to teach himself that language keeping his book propped open on his cobbler's workbench. He discovered that he had a gift for languages and soon learned Hebrew, Latin, French, and Flemish—all self-taught.

He began preaching in a small Baptist church, and for eight years he supported his ministry through his cobbling. And he taped a map of the world above his workbench to remind him to pray for the lost as he worked.

This was at odds with the prevailing thought of his day. Few churches stressed missions; in fact, some theologians taught that the gospel had indeed been carried to all the world, the civilized world that is, and that those who still languished as heathens were obviously under the judgment of God.

Yet Carey's burden for the heathen moved him to speak up at a meeting of ministers, and the moderator replied, "Young man, sit down. When God pleases to convert the heathen He will do it without your aid or mine."

In 1792, Carey published *An Enquiry into the Obligations of Christians to Use Means for the Conversion of the Heathens in Which the Religious State of the Different Nations of the World, the Success of Former Undertakings, and the Practicability of Further Undertakings Are Considered.*

In this book, the fountainhead of the modern missionary movement, Carey argues that the command of Christ to "go into all the world and preach the Gospel" was not restricted to the apostles but is still binding on all Christians.

He also relates the history of previous generations of Christians, such as the Moravian Brethren, who have successfully obeyed the command through difficulties and martyrdom. And he observes that commercial men seeking gain have pushed their way into all corners of the globe "for the profits arising from a few otter-skins." Should Christians do less for "our fellow-creatures whose souls are as immortal as ours?"

He concludes, "Surely it is worth while to lay ourselves out with all our might in promoting the cause and kingdom of Christ."

His small book created a sensation.

Carey was asked to explain his revolutionary ideas to a group of ministers. He used Isaiah 54:2-3 and exhorted Christians to "Expect great things from God; Attempt great things for God."

As a result of his efforts, the Particular Baptist Society For

Propagation Of The Gospel Amongst The Heathen was formed. Carey and John Thomas, a physician, were chosen to go to India as missionaries.

"William, are you mad?" his father said.

"Come what will, I and my children shall remain in England," his wife said.

The East India House said that the captain who dared take the fledgling missionaries aboard a company ship without a permit would find his captain's license revoked.

And the captain who had them on board put them ashore a short distance down the English coast from where they had embarked.

But Carey said, "The sense of duty is so strong as to overpower all other considerations. I can not turn back. . . . All I can say in this affair is that however mysterious the leadings of Providence are, I have no doubt but they are superintended by an infinitely wise God."

The missionaries arranged another passage on a Danish East India ship. During the delay, they convinced Carey's wife and three sons to accompany him. The whole party sailed on the *Kron Princess Maria* on June 13, 1793.

The voyage lasted five months, and when they arrived in Calcutta, British authorities threatened to return them to England on the same ship. But they found refuge in Danish territory.

They discovered that they did not have enough money to live in Calcutta, but Carey found some property at a bargain price on the Hugli River forty miles from the city. No wonder the property came so cheap. Tigers had eaten twenty-six people there in the previous six weeks!

Tigers were the least of Carey's difficulties. For a time, Thomas neglected missionary work to set up a lucrative medical practice in the European community. Carey lamented:

I am in a strange land, alone, no Christian friend, a large family, and nothing to supply their needs. . . . Now all my friends are but One; I rejoice, however, that He is all-sufficient and can supply all my wants, spiritual and temporal. . . . But why is my soul disquieted within me?

When I first left England, my hope of the conversion of the heathen was very strong; but, among so many obstacles, it would die away, unless upheld by God. Nothing to exercise it, but plenty to obstruct it . . . long delays and few opportunities. . . . No earthly thing to depend upon, or earthly comfort, except food and raiment. Well, I have God and his word is sure.

He took a job as manager of an indigo plantation which employed ninety native workers. This work supplied income for his family; it also gave him access, on common ground, to the people of surrounding villages. This contact accelerated his grasp of the language, and soon he was preaching six or eight times a week, in addition to his labor at the plantation.

Malaria sapped his health, and while both he and his wife were bedridden, their five-year-old son died.

No one would bury the child.

The Hindus feared breaking caste, and the Moslems did not want to be contaminated by touching a dead Christian. By the time Carey took care of the burial, his wife had become insane. For the next twelve years, till the time of her death, she raged so violently that she had to be restrained.

And while his wife shrieked and wailed and battered the walls of her room next to his study, William Carey translated the Bible into Bengali, Hindustani and Sanskrit.

By 1825, he was able to report, "The New Testament will soon be printed in thirty-four languages and the Old Testament in eight, besides versions in three varieties of the Hindustani New Testament."

He had translated virtually all of these Bibles himself.

He also prepared grammar books of many Oriental languages so that "with little success those who follow us will [not] have to wade through the same labour that I have in order to stand merely upon the same ground."

But even with all his scholarly work, he was still able to say "preaching the Gospel is the very element of my soul." The Indian people were curious about his activities, yet he complained, "Never were the people more willing to hear, yet more slow to understand. To break the chains of caste a man must endure to be renounced and abhorred by his wife, children, and friends. Every tie that twines around the heart of a husband, father, and neighbor must be torn and broken ere a man can give himself to Christ."

Carey labored thirteen years before seeing the first Indian convert.

He needed help. He prayed, "A large field opens on every side, and millions tormented by ignorance, superstition and idolatry plead with every heart that loves God. Oh, that many laborers may be thrust into the field."

His prayer was answered, and before the end of his career he had established nineteen mission stations throughout India.

But this progress came in the face of every kind of difficulty.

Every change in colonial administration threatened the existence of the mission. Epidemics of cholera killed Europeans and Indians alike by the hundreds of thousands.

The Napoleonic Wars in Europe and the War of 1812 with the United States affected Carey's mission. Ships bearing supplies and money were captured by warring factions. Once a newspaper reporting a new contingent of Baptist missionaries misspelled the word *Baptist;* the government refused them permission to land thinking they were *papist* spies!

At one time there seemed to be a major breakthrough in

preaching. Carey said, "Multitudes used to hang upon the words that came from our lips, and would stand in the thick wedged crowds for hours together in the heat."

But a mutiny by the Indian army caused the government to close the mission presses, to destroy the store of printed tracts and to forbid the missionaries to preach or teach.

You see, most of the Indian army troops were Moslems. A new type of rifle and bullet had been issued to them, but rumor spread that the cartridges were coated with pig fat as a lubricant. Since soldiers had to bite the cartridges to expose the gunpowder inside for firing, and since pork is an abomination to Moslems, the army revolted, disrupting the whole country. And the government tried to halt anything which might upset people more.

That's the reason the mission's apparent breakthrough turned into a disheartening setback almost overnight.

Carey wrote, "Many would see us expelled. We have no security but in God. . . . I have no doubt but that our troubles will tend to the furtherance of the Gospel; but to what extent they may be carried it is impossible to say. . . . We are prepared to suffer in this cause rather than abandon our work."

In the midst of his other work Carey established a leper hospital and several schools. He taught college, received his doctor's degree, edited India's first vernacular newspaper and worked with agricultural experiments to increase India's food supply. He fought slavery, disease, famine and Suttee.

Pressured by Carey, the government abolished Suttee on December 4, 1829. Word arrived at the mission just as Carey was to enter the pulpit to preach his Sunday sermon. Leaving his pulpit to another, he spent the day translating the government edict into the vernacular. He felt that any delay, even a few hours, would have caused more young women to die.

Every January the Hindus kept a festival called *Gunga Sagor.*

In obedience to vows Indian women sacrificed to the Ganges River by throwing their babies to crocodiles. On other occasions they suspended babies in baskets from the branches of holy trees to be eaten by white ants. Carey influenced the authorities to post a British officer and fifty troops at the site of the festival to prevent infant sacrifice.

Carey saw cholera kill fellow workers within two hours of the onset of the first symptoms. He survived a flood which swept away his home. He endured a broken hip, and when the governor sent his personal physician, Carey suffered the cure of "One hundred and ten leeches . . . applied to the thigh." He endured a fire which burned manuscripts of ten versions of the Bible which had taken him years to translate.

In all those things he could say, "I wish to be still and know that the Lord He is God, and to bow to His will in everything. He will no doubt bring good out of this evil and make it promote His interests, but at present the Providence is exceedingly dark."

But his greatest troubles came from other Christians.

During the forty years Carey ministered in India, he always supported the mission through his teaching, managing the indigo plantation, or working as a civil servant. He put eighty per cent of his earnings into the support of the other missionaries and into buying presses, property, paper, and so on to carry on the work.

Toward the end of his life, the Christians who had known him in England were dead. New directors took over the administration of the mission. The new directors and new workers assumed control of all the property Carey had bought. He and the established missionaries on the field felt that they were in a better position to assess the needs of the work and the disposal of the property they themselves had earned.

Carey wrote, "I do not recollect in my whole life anything

which has given me so much distress as this schism. The mission . . . is rent in twain, and exhibits the scandalous appearance of a body divided against itself. We [the old guard] could easily vindicate ourselves, but the vindication would be ours and their disgrace. We have therefore resolved to say nothing, but to leave the matter in God's hands."

And concerning a charge that he was making himself rich at the expense of the work, he answered, "Were I to die today, I should not have property enough for the purchase of a coffin."

Yet another trouble involved his son, Felix, whom he had sent to Burma as a missionary with the advice, "Let the Burmese language occupy your most precious time. . . . Observe a rigid economy. Missionary funds are the most sacred on earth. Cultivate brotherly love. Preach the never failing word of the cross. . . . Be steady in your work and leave the results to God. . . . Shun all indolence and love of ease."

Felix proved to be so industrious that the king of Burma appointed him as an ambassador. Felix resigned from the mission to accept the post and his disappointed father complained, "Felix is shrivelled from a missionary into an ambassador."

But Carey kept on working. When told that an admirer planned to write a book about his life, the elderly Carey said, "If after my removal anyone should think it worth his while to write my life . . . if he give me credit for being a plodder, he will describe me justly. Anything beyond this will be too much. I can plod, I can persevere in any definite pursuit. To this I owe everything."

To William Carey nothing was more important than being a missionary. And among the guidelines he set down for effective work are these: "To set an infinite value on men's souls. . . . To watch for every chance of doing the people good. . . . To be instant in the nurture of personal religion . . . and to preach Christ crucified as the grand means of conversion."

To preach Christ crucified was his goal and when, near his death, he was praised for his linguistic accomplishments, he insisted, "When I am gone, say nothing about Dr. Carey—speak about Dr. Carey's Saviour."

THE PRINCE
OF PREACHERS

Charles Haddon Spurgeon (d. January 31, 1892)

No one suspected that the worship service would end in panic and death.

In fact, the deacons of the New Park Street Chapel in London thought that holding the service in the music hall of Royal Surrey Gardens was "a bold scheme."

Their church building was too small to hold the vast crowds who flocked to hear Charles Haddon Spurgeon, the church's young pastor.

Every Sunday, crowds clogged the streets around the church vying for the tickets needed to get inside. And each Sunday thousands were turned away, disappointed at not being able to hear England's most successful preacher.

To accommodate the crowds, the deacons of the church rented the music hall. A contemporary newspaper describes the hall as London's "largest, most commodious and beautiful building, erected for public amusements, carnivals of wild beasts and wilder men."

On October 19, 1856, people gathered at the hall hours before the preacher was to begin his sermon. Twelve thousand jammed inside; ten thousand others clustered at the outer doors hoping to hear some word from the man called the "Prince of Preachers."

The service began.

A multitude of voices joined in the opening hymn. A deacon led in prayer. Another hymn. Spurgeon mounted the pulpit and surveyed the thousands of expectant faces before him. He read his text and began his opening remarks.

Then it happened.

Somewhere in the crowd a voice screamed a single word—FIRE!

Other people began shouting "FIRE" also. Panic spread as everyone stampeded toward the exits. Men and women shoved and clawed each other to escape.

Those outside heard the commotion and pressed toward the doors to see what was going on inside. Those inside knocked each other down struggling to get out.

People trampled those knocked to the floor. They fought for an inch of space and pulled back those ahead. Mothers dropped their babies, and men smashed out windows with chair legs and clambered through.

There was no fire. Someone had just shouted that to break up the meeting.

Seven people were trampled to death; twenty-eight were hospitalized; scores of others suffered broken bones or were crushed trying to get out of the hall.

Charles Spurgeon was devastated by the tragedy.

He preached to bring men to life in Christ, and he had thought that his extreme popularity was a mark of God's approval. But now, for a time, he felt his popularity had brought death and destruction.

He looked for meaning in what had happened.

He said, "If the Christian did not sometimes suffer heaviness, he would begin to grow too proud, and think too much of himself, and become too great in his own esteem."

Whereas Spurgeon had been known locally as a great preacher before the tragedy, afterward, as news of the event spread, so did his fame. When he resumed preaching two weeks later, even larger crowds gathered to hear him.

But even as his popularity grew so did attacks against him by other preachers and the city's newspapers.

One paper accused him of:

exhibiting that matchless impudence which is his great characteristic, indulging in coarse familiarity with holy things, declaiming in a ranting and colloquial style, strutting up and down the platform . . . and boasting of his own intimacy with heaven with nauseating frequency.

He is a nine day's wonder—a comet that has suddenly shot across the religious atmosphere. He has gone up like a rocket, and ere long will come down like a stick.

It is generally felt that religion is not benefitted by his abnormal proceedings.

The *Saturday Night Review* said, "This hiring of public amusement places for Sunday preaching is a novelty and a painful one. The deplorable accident, in which seven people lost their lives and scores were maimed, mutilated or otherwise cruelly injured, Mr. Spurgeon only considers as an additional intervention of Providence in his favor."

Detractors wanted Spurgeon to give up preaching lest he "preach another crowd into a frenzy of terror—kill and smash a dozen or two more."

But in spite of the opposition of press and jealous clergy—even members of the Baptist Association attacked him—the people of London continued to pour into every meeting where Spurgeon preached.

During the thirty-eight years Spurgeon served the church—which changed its name to the Metropolitan Tabernacle—more people attended there than attended any other church in England—or the world.

Yet Spurgeon, who attracted thousands of hearers, was himself converted at a church where only a handful of people worshiped. And although he earned the title of "Prince of Preachers," he was saved under the ministry of a man who was not a preacher at all.

Charles Spurgeon had been raised in a Christian home; his father was a minister, and his mother a godly woman; but just the same, he needed salvation.

He later said, "I do not hesitate to say that those who examined my life would not have seen any extraordinary sin, yet as I looked upon myself I saw outrageous sin against God.

"If I opened my mouth, I spoke amiss. If I sat still there was sin in my silence. I was in custody of the Law. I dared not plunge into grosser vices; I sinned enough without acting like that."

When he was fifteen years old, he tried to walk to church one winter morning through a blizzard. But the storm raged so harshly that he could not make it to his own church.

He turned down a side street to get out of the wind.

There above the street swayed a snow-encrusted sign—Artillery Street Primitive Methodist Church.

Spurgeon went in to escape the cold.

Only fifteen people had braved the storm to come to church; even the pastor was snowbound and did not show up.

The tiny congregation waited for a time, then started the service without the pastor. They asked a shoemaker to lead them.

The cobbler spoke on Isaiah 45:22: "Look unto me, and be ye saved, all the ends of the earth" (KJV).

He used the example of the repentant thief who was crucified on the cross beside Jesus. That man was nailed down. He could do nothing to earn his salvation. All he could do was look to Jesus to save him. And Jesus promised him, "This day shalt thou be with me in paradise."

When Spurgeon realized that Christ alone is the source of salvation, he later wrote, "The cloud was gone, the darkness rolled away, and in that moment I saw the sun! Oh, I did look. I could have almost looked my eyes away."

That very day Spurgeon decided to enter the ministry.

Over the next months he devoted himself to visiting the poor, handing out tracts and talking with his schoolmates about Christ.

The following May he walked eight miles to be baptized in the River Lark near his home.

He wrote in a letter to his mother, "Conscience has convinced me that it is a duty to be buried with Christ in baptism, although I am sure it constitutes no part of salvation."

He began a Sunday school for other boys while he was still fifteen. He said, "There is no time for work like the first hours of the day and no time for serving the Lord like the earliest days of youth."

He became pastor of a Baptist church in the town of Waterbeach when he was sixteen. The congregation was only twelve people when he started but grew to over a hundred in his two years there.

He hoped to win a conditional scholarship to enter Cambridge University. But when he was to meet the man responsible, a maid showed Spurgeon to the wrong room, and he missed the interview and the scholarship.

He was bitterly disappointed.

That afternoon as he walked in the fields thinking about how he had missed his scholarship, these words of Scripture came to him: "Seekest thou great things for thyself? Seek them not" (Jer 45:5, KJV).

He submitted to God's Word and humbled his heart, telling the Lord that he was willing to remain uneducated, unknown, unsuccessful.

He yielded to God's will in the matter of the scholarship and all else. He became willing to be a nobody if that were God's will for him. He determined to seek glory only for Christ — and never for himself.

Years later, after he had become England's most successful minister, he wrote, "From that day until now I have acted on no other principle but that of perfect consecration to the work whereunto I am called. I surrendered myself to my Saviour. I gave him my body, my soul . . . my whole manhood."

Soon after this, a visiting member of the London church heard Spurgeon speak and suggested that the church call him as pastor. He spent the rest of his life preaching in London.

While he was pastor, 14,700 new members joined the church; 10,800 were baptized there. The church established 49 mission Sunday schools, an orphanage, a newspaper, and a publishing house. Spurgeon wrote 135 books and edited 28 others. Over 3,500 of his sermons were printed, and hundreds of them were translated into many foreign languages. Hundreds of thousands of people were touched by his ministry.

His secret of success?

He said, "I have often found that the place where I have seen most of my own insignificance, baseness, unbelief and depravity has been the place where I have got a blessing. . . ."

"Say much of what the Lord has done for you, but say little of what you have done for the Lord. Do not utter a self-glorifying sentence."

HE HAS A PLAN;
HE HAS
A THRONE

James Hudson Taylor (d. June 3, 1905)

*T*he Chinese barber shaved the young Englishman's head bald except for a long strand of hair at the back that he braided into a pigtail.

When the barber finished, James Hudson Taylor looked like a tall, white-skinned Chinaman. He wore sandals on his feet and the cotton pajama-like clothes and robes of a Chinese teacher.

In the 1850s few foreigners visited China; but when they did, the Chinese distrusted them because they looked so different. They called strangers "foreign devils" or "foreign dogs."

English people in China thought Taylor was crazy for dressing like a native, living among the people and eating with chopsticks. They thought he cheapened the image of an English gentleman in the eyes of the natives.

A more important image concerned Taylor. He did not want the Chinese to notice how he looked; he wanted them to pay attention to what he said; he had come to tell them about Jesus.

Taylor said, "Surely no follower of the meek and lowly Jesus will be likely to conclude that it is beneath the dignity of a Christian missionary to seek identification with this poor people."

More than anything else, Taylor wanted to be a follower of Jesus and to free Chinese people from their guilt.

Taylor wrote, "I feel as if I could not live if something is not done for China. Had I a thousand lives, China should claim every one. No, not China, but Christ."

China had three primary religions—Confucianism, Taoism and Buddhism. The country also contained many adherents to animism who went to pagodas, prayed to idols and burned sticks of incense to their ancestors, but they had never heard that God loves them and that Jesus came to forgive sin. People of all these religions tried to please their gods but never felt clean.

Most worried constantly that demons would get them, so they made the paths leading to their doors crooked—so the demons could not find the way in—and they exploded firecrackers to scare the demons away.

When Taylor first came to China, he got off the boat and walked straight into a war.

He saw soldiers chopping the heads off tied-up enemy prisoners in a crowded marketplace while the Chinese went about their business. Farmers sold pigs. Girls herded flocks of ducks through the crowd. Women with feet so tiny that they could not walk—because their feet had been bound when they were babies—were carried on sedan chairs to market. No one cared about the men being executed.

However it was not the spiritual darkness of China but Taylor's love for Christ that brought him to that strange land.

When James Taylor was a teen-ager he had not been particularly religious. But once, while his parents were gone, he got bored. He picked up a book to read in the hayloft of his father's barn. The book told that on the cross Jesus said the words "It is finished."

Taylor said, "If the whole work was finished, and the whole debt was paid, what is there left for me to do?"

He reasoned that God is so powerful, so rich, that we cannot pay or give him anything. We can only be thankful.

When the teen-ager thought this through, he resolved to live altogether for Christ.

Taylor said, "I besought Him to give me some work to do for Him, as an outlet for love and gratitude . . . Something with which He would be pleased and that I might do directly for Him."

He felt God would give him the privilege of working in China. So Taylor entered medical school to learn practical ways to help sick, hurt people.

While in medical school he came to believe that if he were doing God's work, then God would supply everything he needed. Therefore, when he needed money, food—anything— he told no one but God in prayer.

He followed this practice all his life, and he never lacked for anything.

He said, "No amount of labor and machinery will accomplish without spiritual power, what may be easily accomplished when we place ourselves in the current of God's will and work by His direction, in His way."

Taylor believed that the way to find out God's plan for us is to do everything as service to God.

He said, "Do small things as if they were great, because of

the majesty of Jesus Christ."

We should even, he said, "hang up clothes, wash, dress and comb our hair in a way to use to the full measure of ability which God has given us to the glory of His holy name."

There are three ways to do God's work, Taylor said. We can plan and do our best; we can plan and ask God to bless our plan; or we can ask Christ to show us his plan and obey him.

He said, "God gives his spirit not to those who long for Him, not to those who pray for Him, nor to those who desire to be filled with Him always, but He does give His Holy Spirit to them that obey Him."

Soon after Taylor changed into Chinese dress, he rented a sampan and traveled on the Yangtze River. He slept aboard the houseboat and during the day visited cities and villages preaching, doing medical work, and handing out tracts.

Some people heard the message of Christ gladly. Others tried to kill Taylor.

He saw crocodiles eat people in the river. He saw a man fall from a bridge and drown while none of his Chinese friends moved to help him. He saw idols, slavery, wars, riots, fires, storms, death and trouble everywhere around him. But he kept on working.

He said, "The future is a ravelling [tangled] maze, but my path has always been made plain just one step at a time. I must wait on God and trust in Him and all will be well."

After Taylor married, illness forced him back to England where he founded the China Inland Mission. When he returned to China, several new missionaries accompanied him.

He taught them to adopt native dress, diet and manners, and more importantly, to live trusting God for everything they needed and to "move man through God by prayer alone."

He said, "The apostolic plan was not to raise ways and means but to go and do the work, trusting in His sure word who said,

'Seek ye first the kingdom of God and all these things shall be added unto you.' "

Many people fought what the missionaries were doing.

Taylor described this time saying, "Envied of some, despised by many, hated perhaps by others; often blamed for things I never heard of, or had nothing to do with . . . often sick in body as well as perplexed in mind and embarrassed by circumstances . . . but the battle is the Lord's and He will conquer."

Rioting Chinese throwing bricks attacked the house where the missionaries lived. They set fire to the thatched roof. Several Christians had to jump from upstairs windows to escape, but none were killed.

"We take courage from the goodness of God to us in our extreme peril," Taylor wrote in a letter home.

He believed God was in control, even in the worst situations.

He wrote, "God himself is at the helm, ordering all things after the counsel of his own will. He has a plan and He is carrying it out; He has a throne and that throne rules over all. Our strength then is to sit still and look on."

An epidemic of cholera swept through China. Thousands of people died in the streets. His wife and two of her children also died.

Taylor viewed his wife's death as a joy, an opportunity for her to graduate from this world and to be with Christ; yet he also viewed life down here as a joy to be lived out fully. He expressed these mixed feelings, saying, "I scarcely knew whether she or I was more blessed."

While Taylor was brokenhearted at his wife's death, he kept on working.

In 1887 he prayed for God to send 100 new missionaries to China. He did not ask people to join him—he prayed for them. Over 600 applied to go.

Taylor believed that before we can teach anything about God

we must know that thing ourselves.

He said, "He always gives us the message for ourselves first. . . . He does not send us out with sealed orders."

Taylor believed that faith and knowing God only comes from thinking about him and obeying him. He taught, "How then to have our faith increased? Only by thinking of all that Jesus is, and all He is for us. His life. His death. His work, He himself as revealed to us in the Word.

"It is in the path of obedience and self-denying service that God reveals Himself most intimately to His children."

Once a thief stole all that Taylor owned. Taylor knew the man but decided to obey the Scripture "Do not resist an evil person" (Mt 5:39). He forgave the thief and did not prosecute.

Such behavior led to Taylor's becoming known all over the world as a Christian gentleman. Gifts poured into his mission to replace what he had lost.

A little girl read a book on China he had written years before and wrote to him, "If you have not died since then, I want you to let me know; and I will send you a little money I have saved. . . . Gracie."

Christians everywhere asked him to come teach. He traveled to Scandinavia, Germany, the United States, Australia and India. Thousands flocked to hear him, and hundreds became missionaries themselves.

When Hudson Taylor first went to China, there were only 300 Christians there. After his fifty-one years as a missionary, there were over 100,000 Christians in China.

He was not surprised.

Taylor said, "There is a living God; He has spoken in the Bible; He means what He says, and will do all He has promised."

He had no regrets about his life. He said, "I would not, if I could, be otherwise than I am—entirely dependent upon the

Lord and used as a channel of help to others."

During one of his last sermons, he kept saying one line over and over. Some people thought it was because the old man's mind was slipping. But perhaps he said this because it was the most important thing he had to say, "You can trust the Lord too little, but you can not trust Him too much."

A TITANIC
HERO

Dr. Robert J. Bateman (d. April 14, 1912)

On April 23, 1912, the cable ship *MacKay-Bennet* loaded her strange cargo and set sail from Halifax, Nova Scotia. She carried a preacher, an undertaker, his assistant, a carpenter and 600 empty coffins.

The ship steamed into the North Atlantic to Longitude 50/14 West and Latitude 41/46 North. She cut her speed and began to crisscross the icy water in a thirty-mile square search pattern over water two miles deep.

"Look! There's one over there," the boatswain shouted. The crew lowered a ship's boat and the oarsmen pulled to the spot.

A bloated body, supported by a yellow life jacket, floated in the water. Stenciled on the jacket were the words S.S. *Titanic.* A sailor snagged the lashings on the vest with a boat hook and drew the body over the gunnels. Another sailor attached a metal tag stamped with the numeral 1.

This scene was repeated over and over as the work crew recovered bodies from the ship which had struck an iceberg at 11:45 p.m. on the night of April 14, 1912.

Of the 306 bodies recovered, 190 were identified from the contents of pockets and so on. The body of millionaire John Jacob Astor was found in a suit with a gold belt-buckle and $2,300 in his pocket.

Body number 174 was that of Dr. Robert J. Bateman, a Christian minister from Jacksonville, Florida, the only Floridian to sail on the *Titanic*.

Here is the odd story of how a letter from a prostitute had led the minister to be aboard the ship:

Bateman was the founder and director of the Central City Mission, an outreach for the drunkards and prostitutes in the port's notorious red-light district known as LaVilla, or the Jacksonville Tenderloin. There, tattoo parlors, sleazy bars, whorehouses, pawn shops, flophouses and shops selling everything from knives to live alligators catered to drunken sailors' every need or whim.

Some lines from a poem Bateman wrote describe the area:
Foul Tenderloin, least wholesome spot in town,
Where vice and greed full many a man brings down . . .
Vile hovels of licentiousness and lees,
Haunts of base youth from which virtue flees;
How many hide behind your gaudy screen,
Where hollow happiness befouls each scene?
The dancers there, filled from foaming cup,
Attempting each to hold the other up . . .
These are your "charms" dank section!
Sports like these, that on the morning after fail to please.
Bateman had been born in Bristol, England, on October 14,

1859, but he came to the United States as a young man interested in rescue mission work. He laid the bricks to build the walls of the Central City Mission himself, and when questioned about working so hard, he said, "I had rather have my mission than the best church in America."

A newspaper account of him said, "He stood ever ready to save fallen women—to secure homes for them and rescue them from lives of misery and degradation."

But Bateman saw the scope of his mission as much larger. He said, "The object of this work is to visit the sick, visit the jail, visit the workhouse, feed the poor, clothe the needy, hold nightly meetings, provide a home for fallen girls, an employment bureau, free reading room, visit hospitals, the distribution of religious literature, encourage temperance, help restore lost relatives, and send the wanderer home."

One minister said of the mission, "If Jesus Christ had been in Jacksonville, He would have been seen often at the Central City Mission."

Another went so far as to compare Bateman with Jesus, saying, "He went about doing good. He gathered in the sin-scarred brood, the poor, broken ones, penniless, homeless, helpless, hungry and in rags. He housed the homeless. He fed the hungry. He clothed the naked. He helped the helpless to help themselves."

One monthly report of Bateman's work reads, "836 men given beds, and 1,284 meals were furnished . . . 182 men were sent to work . . . twelve poor families were aided, five wayward girls were sent to the Rescue Home, and homes were found for four boys and three babies—the latter being waifs left on the mission steps."

His contemporaries called him "the man who distributes more human sunshine than any other in Jacksonville."

He moved in the city's highest social circles yet, according to

Edward F. Ley, chairman of the Jacksonville Ministerial Association, "He hob-knobbed with the desolate Magdalenes, the malodorous pitiable tramps, the wandering friendless hobos, the poor besotted drunkards—all children of misfortune."

His contact with both the highest and lowest elements of society led to his death.

Dear Dr. Bateman:

I hear you are going to start a home for us girls. I want to come to it. . . . I can't do anything that is worth anything to anybody. I have tried to leave here but nobody will give me work. . . . This place is terrible and I know lots of girls will come. For God's sake do something quick.

From a Certain House on Davis Street

When Bateman received this letter from a girl in a notorious house near the waterfront docks, he felt he had to help. He contacted a wealthy Northern patron of the mission, who promised to help finance a home for fallen women and who paid for Bateman to go to England to study the methods used in the orphanage founded by George Muller of Bristol, who was known worldwide for his innovative social work and prayer life.

Bateman hoped to reorganize his rescue mission along the same lines as the orphanage. He always carried an autographed picture of Muller in his watchcase.

One daily newspaper said, "Dr. Bateman has been making a tour of study and observation in England for the purpose of familiarizing himself with the best methods of lifting fallen humanity."

Another said, "A mission of mercy . . . in behalf of the fallen women and drunkards of the Southland."

While yet another termed his trip "a tour of investigation to the hotbeds of iniquity in London, England."

While touring the hotbeds, the doctor also conducted revival services in English churches.

When he preached in Bristol, he usually closed the service with his favorite hymn, "Nearer My God to Thee." His preaching was so popular that upon his departure a band playing that same hymn escorted him and Mrs. Ada Ball, his sister-in-law, to the train which would take them to the *Titanic* for the trip back to America.

The *Titanic* was the world's largest and most luxurious ship. She was 882.5 feet long with a gross tonnage of 46,328 tons. On this, her maiden voyage, the *Titanic* carried 2,207 people. Enjoying first-class accommodations were the cream of American and Continental society. The first-class passengers were estimated to be collectively worth over $500,000,000.

Bateman and Mrs. Ball traveled second class.

All passengers traveled in comfort, luxury—and security. "With her numerous watertight compartments she is absolutely unsinkable and it makes no difference what she hit," said P. A. Franklin, highest New York official of the White Star Line.

Edward J. Smithe, the *Titanic*'s captain, said, "I cannot imagine any condition which would cause a ship to founder. Modern shipbuilding has gone beyond that."

"God Himself could not sink this ship," boasted one of the deckhands.

According to Mrs. Ball's later statements, on Sunday, April 14, 1912, Bateman conducted the only religious service held aboard the liner. He concluded the service with the hymn "Nearer My God to Thee." She said that he seemed extremely happy and walked about the ship singing to himself that day.

That same night at 11:45 p.m., an iceberg grazed the side of the *Titanic*. The ice peeled a 300-foot strip from the steel hull.

Mrs. Ball said after her rescue, "For some time we had been seeing icebergs of various sizes floating in the ocean. Despite this fact, the ship was running at a tremendous rate of speed."

Different people experienced the collision differently according to where they were on the huge ship when the iceberg struck and depending on whether or not the person was awake or asleep at the time. For instance, one passenger said the sound of the metal being stripped from her side sounded no louder than a strip of cloth being torn. On the other hand, Mrs. Ball's cabinmate, Mrs. A. S. Jerwan, said, "It was a tremendous shock that made me think the boilers had blown up."

Mrs. Ball was asleep. Her cabinmate woke her. "I laughed at her and told her there was nothing wrong and went back to sleep," Mrs. Ball said.

Bateman pounded on the door to the women's stateroom.

There was no time to dress. Mrs. Ball ventured onto the boat deck in her nightgown. The arctic cold of that night made her want to go back inside, but Bateman took off his overcoat and draped it around her shoulders.

The *Titanic* carried lifeboats sufficient for less than half the number of people on board.

As Bateman escorted the ladies to one of the boats, he said to his sister-in-law, "Don't be nervous, Annie, This will test our faith. I must stay and let the women go. If we never meet again on this earth, we will meet again in Heaven."

She said, "As the boat lowered, Robert stepped to the railing and threw me his silk handkerchief. 'Put that around your throat,' he said, 'You'll catch cold.' Just imagine thinking of such a little thing in a time like that."

Confusion and turmoil ruled in the lifeboat. Mrs. Jerwan said, "I found a baby in my possession without the least idea whom it belonged to. I never did find out. . . . Our boat had more children in it than any of the others."

A surviving passenger said, after he saw his sister-in-law safely off the ship, that Bateman "collected about fifty men on the stern of the ship and told them that they should prepare for death. And he led them in praying the Lord's Prayer."

Mrs. Ball's lifeboat remained near the *Titanic*. She believed that Bateman persuaded the band to play "Nearer My God to Thee" in the *Titanic*'s last moments.

She said, "Before we had been in the boat very long we saw the Titanic go down. . . . The stars were bright and we could see the lights of the ship. The band was on the stern and went down playing. We could hear the screams of those on board and cries of 'Save Us' but of course we could do nothing."

As the bow of the ship filled with water, the stern rose higher and higher till the *Titanic* stood nearly perpendicular to the icy Atlantic. The lights of the ship remained on, even in the already submerged bow giving a rosy submarine glow. Those in the lifeboats could see men clinging to handholds "like clusters of bees on a tree."

Then the ship slid under.

Hundreds of men struggled in the freezing water. Ada Ball said, "Many swam in different directions. We could only see those nearest our boat. I saw at least 200 bodies in the water."

She also said that she saw a man in another lifeboat shooting at swimmers to keep them away so they could not swamp the boat he was in.

The women spent seven hours in the lifeboat, which had sprung a plank when it hit the water. They bailed all night to keep from being swamped, and they burned handkerchiefs and strips of clothing for warmth and light.

The first rescue ship arrived at dawn.

Of the 2,207 aboard the *Titanic*, only 705 survived. After treatment at Sydenham Hospital in New York, Mrs. Ball went to Jacksonville to stay with her sister.

Ten days after the disaster, the widow received a letter from her dead husband. Bateman had written on shipboard and mailed the letter in Ireland when the *Titanic* had stopped for more passengers.

He had written, "I feel that my trip has not been in vain. God has singularly blessed me. We had a glorious revival. . . . It was the Time of My Life."

When the family pried open Bateman's locked desk, they found that he had written checks to cover the next month's bills. He had also written a poem on a black-bordered card and left it on top of his papers:

Do you shudder as you picture
All the horrors of that hour?
Ah! But Jesus was beside me
To sustain me by His power.

And He came Himself to meet me
In that way so hard to tread
And with Jesus' arm to cling to
Could I have one doubt or dread?

His nephew also received a letter from Bateman which had been mailed from the *Titanic*'s stop in Ireland. Bateman had written, "Tom, if this ship goes to the bottom, I shall not be there, I shall be up yonder. Think of it!"

MARY
AND THE
BEANSTALK

Mary Slessor of Calabar (d. January 13, 1915)

Scores of upset, sullen African warriors surrounded Presbyterian missionary Mary Slessor. Some rattled ironwood spears against their rhinoceros-hide shields. Some shook clubs in the lone woman's face. Others swung broad, flat-ended swords over her head. All screamed and shouted at her.

Still she would not give them back their beans.

She marched through the ranks of screaming, drunken warriors to her mud hut, carried the sack of beans inside, shut the door and went to bed.

All night the warriors milled around outside her door, drinking more trade rum, cursing and wondering what to do about the bag of beans.

This encounter took place in 1890 near the mouth of the

Calabar River in Calabar, Africa, a country on the west coast just north of the equator.

It was one of many confrontations between Mary Slessor and armed tribesmen over beans. They also faced off in confrontation over twins, women, slavery, intertribal war, justice, and the gospel of Jesus Christ.

Yet, her contemporaries described the Scottish girl as a wee lassie so shy that she got stage fright and avoided public speaking.

But God gave her a holy boldness for working in one of the most challenging mission fields on earth.

Calabar, the Slave Coast of Africa, took its geographic names from the area's two most notable features: slavery and the Calabar bean.

The Africans of the Slave Coast continued to enslave each other long after Europe and the United States abolished slavery. Strong tribes captured weak ones and sold them to still other tribes or to Arab slave traders.

Use of the poisonous Calabar bean also shaped the area's culture.

The brown bean grows in pods about six inches long. Nothing in the bean's taste, smell or appearance distinguishes it from other beans. The difference is discovered after it is eaten.

Then the bean's chemical increases the output of the victim's salivary glands as it constricts the blood vessels leading to those glands. Blood pressure rises. Violent vomiting begins. The person dies a prolonged, messy death as the poison affects the functions of virtually all body organs. Tremors and convulsions of the spinal cord set in. Yet, mental functions are not affected; the victim remains conscious of what is happening to him during all this. Finally, the person's lungs become waterlogged; death follows as the victim drowns in his own spit.

Feeding sacrificial victims the Calabar bean and watching the ensuing show comprised a major part of the country's religious heritage.

Four other elements characterized the religious animism of the area: fear of JuJu, evil spirits believed to reside in trees, rocks and animals; fear of witchcraft; fear of secret societies, known as Egbo; and fear of dying alone.

These fears expressed themselves as cruelty.

For instance, the tribes believed that all sickness is evil and comes from a devil. Therefore, whenever a person got sick or died, then obviously the trouble was the result of a witch sicking a demon on the sufferer. This crime called for a bean trial.

In the trial, the chief or witch doctor forced the accused witches to eat the bean. Innocent people did not go into convulsions; the guilty did. Of course, only the witch doctor who picked the beans could tell which kind of plant a particular bean came from originally.

These trials became an almost daily affair.

Another way the religious fears of the people came out in daily life was in their burial customs. The more important the dead man, the higher the number of wives and slaves who were strangled at his graveside to be buried with him.

A third expression of animism's fears lay in the people's dread of twins. They believed that a human man could only begat one child at a time. Therefore, if a woman gave birth to twins, that meant she had been having intercourse with a demon.

A living twin was thought to be a demon incarnate who could bring disaster on the whole tribe. The gods, good taste and public well-being demanded that these abominations be exterminated. Newborn twins were immediately stuffed into clay pots and left outside the villages for ants to eat.

Notice that just about all of these cruelties primarily involved women. Women, even those who were not outright slaves, were the property of their fathers or husbands. When a girl reached a marriageable age, she was placed in seclusion and fattened to increase her bride price. Once married, she lived in a harem with her husband's other wives.

When the Egbo societies raided a village, the women were beaten and degraded in wild orgies. When a husband died, the wives were strangled and buried with him. Half his wives were buried below his body and half above in the common grave. When witchcraft was suspected in illness or accident, women were accused first. When twins were born, when slaves were captured, when warriors got drunk on trade rum, the women suffered.

Yet, the women were more cruel to each other than the men!

This was especially true in the treatment of slaves and in the treatment of newer wives brought into the harem. And no one was more likely to accuse a woman of witchcraft and call for the bean trial than her own sisters in the compound.

Other charms of Calabar included wild elephant herds, which periodically tore down the grass and mud huts of the villages; millions of driver ants which defoliated trees, eating everything in their path; poisonous snakes of every size and description; crocodiles in the rivers that snapped up anyone who fell out of a canoe; and hippopotamus herds in those same rivers which capsized said canoes.

Why in the world would a lady want to leave home in civilized Scotland and go to a place like Calabar?

What could keep her there for thirty-nine years as a missionary? Why would she choose to spend several of her vacation times going deeper into the bush rather than returning home?

Mary Slessor said, "God has been good to me, letting me serve Him in this humble way. I cannot thank Him enough for the honor He conferred upon me when He sent me to the Dark Continent."

Mary Slessor had been converted as a child in Dundee, Scotland, where her father was an abusive drunk and her mother a factory worker. When she was eleven years old, Mary began working twelve-hour shifts at the looms in the textile mill.

Her background made her both tough and tender in the right proportions.

During her off-time from the mills, she helped teach a slum Sunday-school Bible class for the Presbyterian church. She also engaged in open-air meetings, though she was too shy to speak herself. The exploits of David Livingstone in Africa excited her devotion, and for fourteen years she worked in the factory, learned to read, taught the slum children and prayed to become a missionary.

She learned about conditions in Calabar through reading the *Missionary Record,* a magazine which in later years published many of her own letters and reports. In 1874, Livingstone died and the next year Mary Slessor volunteered to the Scottish Missionary Society. She sailed for Calabar in 1876.

For the next twelve years she worked in the towns near the mouth of the Calabar River where she mastered the language, learned the customs of the place, grew spiritually, prayed and assisted senior missionaries.

She said, "Blessed the man or woman who is able to serve cheerfully in the second rank. . . . The test of a real good missionary is this waiting, silent, seemingly useless time."

She believed that the ordinary is as important to the kingdom of God as the dramatic. She said, "Everything, however seemingly secular and small, is God's work for the moment and worthy of our very best endeavor."

She longed to engage in pioneer missionary work, to open new territories. Yet, she looked for God's time.

"Christ was never in a hurry. There was no rushing forward, no anticipating, no fretting over what might be. Every day's duties were done as every day brought them, and the rest was left with God. 'He that believeth shall not make haste,' " she said.

In 1888, when she was forty years old, the opportunity opened for her to travel upriver by canoe into the bush country to minister to the Okyong tribe. Circumstances dictated that she was the only missionary to enter that area. Because of the heat, this trip, like most of her travels in Africa, was travelled through the jungle at night.

When she arrived the village was deserted.

All the people were at a funeral. The chief's mother had died, and when he returned he happily reported to the new missionary that he had given the old lady a grand send-off by killing twenty-four people to be buried with her. Also, four "witches" had died in the bean trial, proving they had been responsible for her death.

Mary Slessor wrote, "The tribe seemed so completely given over to the devil that we were tempted to despair."

In order to win the people to Christ, Mary Slessor abandoned her European clothing and dressed in the Calabar national costume. She ate the same food as the people she taught and drank unpurified water.

These practices injured her health, but she felt that the more she could identify with the people, the more they could focus on the content of her teachings.

She said, "It is a real life I am living now, not all preaching and holding meetings, but rather a life and an atmosphere which the people can touch and live in and be made willing to believe in when the higher truths are brought before them."

She built her own hut to live in out of sticks and mud. Her bed was a mat on the floor, and she made cupboards, table and even chairs out of mud molded into shape and dried.

She said, "In a home like mine, a woman can find infinite

happiness and satisfaction. It is an exhilaration of constant joy—I cannot fancy anything to surpass it on earth."

Why could she be happy in such a place?

She said, "Life is so great and so grand; and eternity is so real and so terrible in its issues. . . . All is dark, except above. Calvary stands safe and sure. . . . Life apart from Christ is a dreadful gift.

"Christ is here and the Holy Spirit, and if I am seldom in a triumphant or ecstatic mood, I am always satisfied and happy in His love."

One of the first things she did in her new home was to begin collecting twin babies. She literally gathered castaway babies off the village trash piles. She raised dozens of sets of twins in her home. For years she was seldom without a baby in her arms, whatever else she might be doing.

A crisis descended on the village when a falling log crushed the chief's son during construction of a house.

Mary nursed the young man for days, but he died anyhow and the tribe prepared for a funeral. People cowered, wondering who would be sacrificed to be buried with him.

Mary wanted to keep anyone from being buried with him, so she devised a strange plan.

She insisted on preparing the body herself. She bathed the dead man and dressed him in the finest European clothes she could find in the mission box. She tied silk scarves around him, gave him a fancy haircut, painted his face yellow, and crowned him with a top hat. Then she sat the body upright in a chair, with a whip and a cane in his hands. She fastened a large umbrella over the chair and anchored a mirror in front. Then she called the chief and all the people to come see.

By giving the prince such an elaborate send-off herself, she hoped to persuade the chief away from sacrificing people in the grave. Her bizarre ploy worked through five stages.

First, while everyone admitted the funeral display was a wonder, they still felt at least twelve people ought to go into the grave. A bean trial was scheduled for two days later.

Second, Mary prayed intensely. She said:

My life is one long daily, hourly, record of answered prayer. For physical health, for mental over strain, for guidance given marvelously, for errors and dangers averted, for enmity to the Gospel subdued, for food provided at the exact hour needed, for everything that goes to make up life and my poor service. . . . It [prayer] is the very atmosphere in which I live and breathe and have my being, and it makes life glad and free and a million times worth living. I can give no other testimony.

The third stage in the proceedings happened the evening before the prince's funeral. Two missionary visitors chanced to come upriver to call on Mary. They brought with them a magic lantern (which was a sort of pre-electric slide projector). In honor of the dead man they showed London street scenes!

This display pleased the crowd as the most magnificent send-off a dead prince had ever had. They now agreed to place only one cow and one witch in his grave.

At the fourth stage of things, Mary convinced them to chain the witch in her house until the funeral. They agreed. Her house was considered an unholy place because of the twin babies she kept there, but the warriors remained hell-bent on giving the accused woman the bean trial. More people gathered from all over the district as word of the strange burial spread. Warriors tapped keg after keg of trade rum.

Tension mounted. The poison beans were prepared.

Finally, the fifth act of this drama occurred when the shy little Scottish woman marched out of her hut, snatched the bag of beans away from the chief, and stood his armed warriors down face to face.

The prince was buried in style, but without any company save the cow. It was the first funeral in the tribe's history with no human sacrifices.

Such confrontations grew common. One lone woman and Christ against an army.

Once she halted an intertribal war by marching between the two opposing armies and demanding they pile their weapons at her feet. She collected a heap of spears, bows, arrows, clubs and knives five feet high!

Was the missionary fearless?

Of course not. She said, "I had often a lump in my throat and my courage repeatedly threatened to take wings and fly away—though nobody guessed it."

Was she faithful?

She said, "If I have done anything in my life, it has been easy because the master has gone before."

Once she was traveling to a new village with a group of her baby twins. Thirty-three men paddled the huge canoe when a hippopotamus attacked. Dozens of men dove overboard to escape. Mary would not leave her babies. She grabbed a tin dishpan from the supplies and frantically pounded the beast on the head—*Boing! Boing! Boing!*—as it tried to bite the canoe in half.

The startled hippo knew it had bitten off more than it could chew; it swam away, with its ears ringing no doubt.

Mary said, "I don't live up to half the ideal of missionary life. It is not easier to be a saint here than at home. We are very human and not goody-goody at all."

Her holy boldness earned the respect of the people; more and more of them turned to Christ.

A hymn she taught the people sums up her message:
Jesus the son of God came down to earth.
He came to save us from our sins.
He was born poor that He might feel for us.

Wicked men killed Him and hanged Him on a tree.

He rose and went to heaven to prepare a place for us. . . .
Mary Slessor began building churches in the architectural style
familiar to the tribes.

She said, "We don't begin, or end either, with a house; we
begin and end with God in our hearts."

When a notorious bad guy came to a service, she chased him
out, yelling, "God has no need of the likes of you with your
deceit and craft. He can get on quite well without you—though
you can't get on without God. Ay, you have that lesson to learn
yet!"

The congregation cheered.

Once, returning from furlough in Scotland, she packed her
bags with cement powder, the only way she had to transport it.

She used the cement for church and mission buildings deep
in the bush, but she had no training in cement work.

She said, "I just stir it like porridge; turn it out, smooth it with
a stick, and all the time keep praying, 'Lord, here's the cement;
if to Thy glory, set it,' and it has never once gone wrong."

Besides all this, she raised over fifty abandoned babies. She
felt that Christian missions demand women tough and tender.
She called for women to join missionary work:

Consecrated, affectionate women who are not afraid of work
or of filth of any kind, moral or material . . . women who can
tactfully smooth over a roughness and for Christ's sake bear
a snub, and take any place which may open. Women who can
take everything to Jesus and there get strength to smile and
persevere and pull on under any circumstances. If they can
play Beethoven and paint and draw and speak French and
German so much the better, but we can want all these latter
accomplishments if they have only a loving heart, willing
hands, and common sense.

When the new invention of radio came on the scene, Mary

Slessor drew parallels between radio receivers and the Christian life, saying, "We can only obtain God's best by fitness of receiving power. Without receivers fitted and kept in order, the air may tingle and thrill with the message, but it will not reach my spirit and consciousness."

She constantly strove to be tuned in and receive from God.

Yet, she knew the frustration of not seeing prayers answered to her immediate satisfaction. She wrote a friend,

I know what it is to pray for long years and never get an answer—I had to pray for my father. But I know my heavenly Father so well that I can leave it with Him for the lower fatherhood. . . .

You thought God was to hear and answer you by making everything straight and pleasant—not so are nations or churches or men and women born; not so is character made. God is answering your prayer in His way. . . . The gate of heaven is never shut.

For a time she was engaged to marry another missionary, but they broke off their engagement when he decided to work in another field. She lived and worked alone most of her life.

Because she was tough but fair, she became the only White person many of the tribes trusted. The British colonial government recognized her stature and appointed her as district judge.

On being appointed to the bench she said, "It will be a good chance to preach the Gospel and to create confidence and inspire hope in these poor wretches who fear white and black man alike; while it will neither hamper my work nor restrict my liberty."

By demonstrating a better way than the bean test to try every crime from chicken snatching to murder, she influenced the eventual abandonment of ordeal by beans.

Her letters and reports to the *Missionary Record* magazine

earned her worldwide fame. In her day she became as famous as David Livingstone had been in his. Donations poured in for her work, and she used the money to build homes for abandoned twins, a home for battered wives and a hospital. Many of the twins she had rescued as infants she saw grow to adulthood, marry, go to college or become Christian workers.

Not only did the tribes and the colonial government honor her, but King George V awarded her the Order of the Hospital of St. John of Jerusalem. She kept the honor secret from her fellow missionaries until telegrams of congratulation began pouring in from all over the world.

She said, "I have lived my life very quietly and in a very natural and humble way. It isn't Mary Slessor doing anything, but Something outside of her altogether uses her as her small ability allows."

She felt uncomfortable being addressed as Lady Slessor and said, "I am Mary Mitchell Slessor, nothing more and none other than the unworthy, unprofitable—but most willing—servant of the King of Kings."

THE WORST
PEOPLE
ON EARTH

Five martyred by the Aucas (d. January 8, 1956)

*U*ntil January 8, 1956, few people had heard of the Auca Indians of Ecuador. They were just another backwater primitive tribe scratching out a mean existence in jungle clearings. But on that day on a sandbar in a river near two Auca villages, two alien cultures—one dedicated to spreading the gospel of Christ, the other to war and murder—clashed. And the Aucas' murder of five American missionaries catapulted the tribe into world-wide news.

Life photographer Cornell Capa accompanied the team which buried the missionaries on the sandbar where they had been killed. He reported, "Among the effects of the missionaries . . . were three diaries in which the men had recorded, step by step, the progress of their mission."

In these diaries, notebooks and letters to their families, the missionaries reveal their motives for jeopardizing their lives among the Aucas.

Time magazine called the Aucas "the worst people on earth."

They were, the magazine said, "A pure Stone Age people, they hate all strangers, live only to hunt, fight and kill. Their most notable products are needle-sharp, 9-foot, hardwood spears for use against human foes. . . . Even their neighbors, the Jivaros, famous for shrinking human heads, live in constant fear of the fierce Aucas."

Murder was the most significant cause of death among the Aucas. Seventy-four per cent of all Auca men died through violent tribal warfare.

When one of their number got sick or old, his relatives dug a pit beneath his hammock, toppled him in and buried him alive.

The tribe suffered a shortage of women because mothers often strangled girl babies with a vine as soon as they were born. One Auca mother of twins said, "I was so frightened to see two babies appear, instead of just one, that I buried them."

The Aucas killed for sport, lust, jealousy or out of simple irritation. One Indian speared both his friend's wife and mother to death as a joke.

As soon as an Auca boy could walk, his spear practice began. Toddlers jabbed short spears into a balsa-wood log carved in human shape. Six-year-olds accompanied men on raids. The adults incapacitated a victim and encouraged the little boys to finish him off.

Murder for revenge and preventative murder also played a large part in the Aucas' lifestyle. They felt it a duty to avenge the murder of a relative by spearing the killer or any member of his family, even a distant cousin.

Therefore, when an Auca suspected that someone might

hold a grudge against some member of his family, he endeavored to kill that person first.

Against such a background it is easy to understand how fear of outsiders and overwhelming suspicion of anything beyond their control motivated the Aucas to spear the five peaceful missionaries when the two cultures met. The drive which motivated the young Americans to expose themselves to such an attack may be more difficult to understand.

The five men represented several Christian denominations and three different mission groups.

Nathaniel Saint of Huntington Valley, Pennsylvania, flew as a pilot for the Mission Aviation Fellowship. Roger Youderian of Lansing, Michigan, served under the Gospel Missionary Union. James Elliot of Portland, Oregon, Pete Fleming of Seattle, Washington, and T. Edward McCully of Milwaukee, Wisconsin, worked for Christian Missions In Many Lands.

Nate Saint, while a maintenance crew chief in the Air Force, decided to become a missionary at a New Year's Eve church service in Detroit.

He wrote, "It was the first time I had ever really heard that verse, 'Follow me and I will make you to become fishers of men.' The old life of chasing things that are of a temporal sort seemed absolutely insane."

After his discharge from the Air Force, he joined Mission Aviation Fellowship as a pilot.

While Ed McCully attended law school at Marquette University, he worked as a night-desk clerk at a hotel. During the slack hours before dawn he read the Bible.

He wrote, "On the way home yesterday morning, I took a long walk and came to a decision which I know is of the Lord. I have one desire now—to live a life of reckless abandon for the Lord, putting all my energy and strength into it. . . . If there's nothing to this business of eternal life we might as well lose everything in one crack and throw our present life away with our life hereafter. But if there is something to it. . . . Well, that's it."

Roger Youderian had jumped, as a paratrooper, into the Battle of the Bulge. He was decorated for his part in the fighting. In a letter to his mother he said, "Ever since I accepted Christ as my personal Saviour last fall and wanted to follow Him and do the will of the Lord, I've felt the call to either missionary, social or ministerial work after my release from the service. . . . I want to be a witness for Him and live following Him every second of my life."

Youderian's call led him to work among the head-hunting Jivaros, and he developed a technique using drawings to teach them to read and write in their own previously unwritten language.

Youderian went through some deep physical and spiritual struggles, but, concerning divine guidance his diary records, "The Holy Spirit can and will guide me in direct proportion to the time and effort I will expend to know and do the will of God."

Pete Fleming had been converted at age thirteen through the testimony of a blind evangelist. When he chose to become a missionary, he had already earned his master's degree in literature and was majoring in philosophy at the University of Washington. Concerning his decision to go to Ecuador, he wrote, "A call is nothing more or less than obedience to the will of God as God presses it home to the soul by whatever means He chooses."

As he decided to move from work among the relatively peaceful Quichuas to the warlike Aucas he said, "It is a grave and solemn problem; an unreachable people who murder and kill with extreme hatred. It comes to me strongly that God is leading me to do something about it, and a strong idea and impression comes into my mind that I ought to devote the majority of my time to collecting linguistic data on the tribe. . . . I know that this may be the most important decision of my life, but I have a quiet peace about it."

The fifth missionary, Jim Elliot, wrote to a friend mentioning his motive for being a missionary: "The command is plain; you go into the whole world and announce the good news. . . . To me, Ecuador is simply an avenue of obedience to the simple word of Christ. There is room for me there, and I am free to go. . . . The will of God is always a bigger thing than we bargain for."

The Auca tribe came to the attention of the missionaries when two Indian survivors of an Auca raid staggered into a mission station. Saint described the victims before he flew them to a hospital:

> The woman was being carried on a bamboo stretcher and had a serious-looking lance puncture under the armpit. They told us that the lance broke off in the wound. Her attacker was going to jab at her again but she grabbed the end of the lance and hung on to save her life. She is about six or seven months pregnant. The man arrived under his own power although considerably crippled up with chest punctures, a hole all the way through one thigh and a hole through his hand where he had apparently tried to stop one of the deadly shafts.

The missionaries decided to reach the Aucas and began learning rudiments of their language from an Auca woman who had been captured as a slave by another tribe.

They made air drops of gifts useful to the Aucas: copper kettles, red shirts, buttons and small knives. Nate Saint devised a method to exchange items with people on the ground without landing the airplane. As his plane circled, he played out a long rope with a basket tied to the end. Centrifugal force caused the basket to gravitate to the center of the circle as it dropped lower and lower. When the rope was fully extended from the spiraling plane, the basket remained almost stationary a few feet above the ground and trade items or messages could be placed in it.

The missionaries used this method to lower pictures of themselves so the people would recognize them when they landed. And as they flew over villages in the dense jungle, the Americans shouted over the plane's loudspeaker, "We like you. We like you. We are friends."

The Aucas took the gifts and replaced them with fruit, feathered headdresses, live parrots and even a balsa-wood carving of the airplane in exchange. This friendly commerce continued for months before the missionaries hazarded direct contact.

Saint landed the plane on a firm sandbar in the Curaray River at a spot near two Auca villages. The Indians first sent out a nubile young girl, apparently intended as a gift, to meet them. The missionaries nicknamed her Delilah.

She left abruptly.

During a supply flight, Saint spotted a large party of Aucas approaching. He quickly landed, and the missionaries prepared to greet their visitors.

The Aucas attacked.

They skewered the Christians with spears and hacked them down with stolen machetes. In a frenzy they peeled the fabric from the fuselage of the plane and twisted its steel landing struts.

Then they crept back into the jungle to await the massive retaliation which their culture taught them to expect.

It never came.

Instead of bombs, Mission Aviation Fellowship pilots continued to drop trade items on the Auca villages, just as though the attack had never happened.

The widows of the five missionaries asked the outraged

Ecuadorian government not to send the army against the Indians. These women continued to study the language of the Aucas and to pray for access to the tribe.

Within three years Mrs. Jim Elliot, her daughter, Valerie, and Rachel Saint, sister of the pilot, were living in an Auca village teaching the Indians about a forgiving Christ.

Soon a Christian church was established among the Aucas. Nathaniel Saint's son was baptized on the sandbar in the Curaray by an Auca pastor who had once been in the raiding party which martyred his father.

A Mission Aviation Fellowship spokesman said, "About a third of the tribe are baptized believers, and meet weekly in six different settlements for Bible study and prayer.

"In the years since Saint and his fellows were killed, quite a few Christians—I would estimate several thousand in the overall missionary community—have dedicated their own lives to Christ because of the example of these men. M.A.F. constantly gets applications from people who have been inspired by the story. This is still going on right now."

Epilog

Who Is Next?

*T*he bum's approach mixed caution with disturbing boldness. He blundered his way through the people on the street
like a stray dog—hungry, but leery of getting another kick.

He kept his eyes downcast, looking at the ground six inches
in front of his dirty, mismatched tennis shoes. Occasionally he
would glance up, seeking eye contact with some passerby.
When he detected a gleam of acknowledgment or sympathy, he
shuffled up to that person and mumbled, "Got a little spare
change I can have?"

He acted satisfied with whatever little bit he received. He
demanded nothing. He asked for little. He expected little.

Jesus Christ is not a bum.

Can you imagine him sidling up to you, begging for a little

bit of your spare change, time or attention?

Never!

He comes in like he owns the place.

He moves through lives in the manner of one exercising his hereditary right of proprietary. When he wanted a donkey, he told his servants to untie one, and if the owner objected merely to say, "The Lord has need of him." He called a tax collector away from his desk in the middle of a workday. At his order commercial fishermen abandoned their nets on the drying racks and their boat on the beach. And when one man pleaded that he needed to go to his father's funeral, Jesus said, "Follow me, and let the dead bury their own dead" (Mt 8:22).

Following Jesus is what made the people in this book different from others. Aside from that, each of them was exactly like the rest of us. They had the same ambitions, dreams, plans and problems we do. In following him they became original individuals in ways they would not have realized had they lived out their own plans. Contact with him changed them. They became, in varying degrees, like him.

You and I also have that potential.

A knife blade or hammerhead—anything made of iron and rubbed against a magnet—gains magnetism. Yet it retains its individuality. A knife blade does not become something else; it holds its cutting edge *and* it becomes magnetic. It is still itself, but now it has something extra.

In some ways godliness seems to work like that. Drawing close to the magnet that is Jesus, we become more like him and at the same time have our unique individuality enhanced. But the analogy breaks down because iron acts according to its nature. We act according to ours.

And our nature resists the pull of God. We Christians don't fully trust him. Not in the things that matter—such as our everyday lives. We are reluctant to make a full commitment, to take a chance. We do not want to be changed. We feel little need for change. We fight change. I'm quite comfortable just as I am, thank you.

Besides, I'm afraid.

What if Jesus called me to do something embarrassing, like Francis on the church steps or Taylor with his Chinese haircut? What if he required me to speak before multitudes like Spurgeon? What if he wants us to limit our self-defined talents by ministering primarily to our own family like Susannah Wesley? Suppose he tells me to go to a far country to live and die among strangers, as the missionaries in this book did?

What would happen if I followed Jesus without reservation? What kind of person would I be?

When Jesus calls us, we would feel more comfortable about following if we knew exactly where he was going. If we knew that, then we could pick and choose. We could exercise our intelligence and negotiate a contract with him on our terms. It's only reasonable to ask where he is going before we agree to tag along.

"If anyone would come after me, he must deny himself and take up his cross and follow me," he said (Mt 16:24).

We are to carry a cross when we follow Jesus, because he is leading us to a crucifixion—ours.

Where did we expect him to lead us?

Are servants any better than their Lord? Can we expect better treatment in this world than he received?

Of course we want to avoid pain, death and even inconvenience. Who doesn't? But these things are inevitable whether or not we follow Jesus. If we do not die first, then we face senility. All our personal plans are bound to come to naught. In the long run, we will not have our own way—even if we never give Jesus another thought.

There are two further factors to consider.

The first is that this world will not last forever; we will.

We were not made to exist permanently in this world. We are passing through here—temporary residents, strangers on the earth.

Like caterpillars destined to fly in the air and drink nectar, we were born to soar—not to remain in our present state, sealed in our self-woven cocoons.

We will spend all eternity somewhere. We will continue forever in the presence of Jesus or we will . . . Well, the alternative is not something we want to think about.

The second factor to consider is the character of Jesus Christ.

If you are dealing with a bum asking for a little something from you, then you can treat him this way or that according to how you feel. If you are dealing with a king's command, then it's an entirely different matter.

Throughout Scripture Jesus is identified as King of kings and Lord of lords, the Prince of Peace, the Ancient of Days, the Mighty God, Emmanuel—God enfleshed and come to earth.

He is these things or he is not.

The people whose biographies you have read believed that he was indeed all he claimed to be and that he put aside such majesty to enter this world, that he lowered himself even to become human, that he served such as us even to washing his disciples' feet, and that he voluntarily allowed himself to be executed as a common criminal because of the love in his own nature.

They were further convinced that because he is the Lord of life, Jesus resumed life after his crucifixion and forty days later returned home to the place he had come from, and that he will come here again, bringing the curtain down on this world.

Because the saints acknowledged these things, they reacted with love for him and gratitude for what he is and what he has done. Most of their actions can be seen simply as expressions of appreciation.

They valued him.

They recognized that they were themselves pilgrims and strangers on the earth and that he is its maker, master and means of support.

The saints were what they were only because of their evaluation of him.

And you and I make that same evaluation—or some other evaluation—every single day we live. Now, either Jesus Christ is worth serving with all our mind and heart, or he isn't.

If Jesus is king rather than bum, his call to us is not a humble, timid plead for a handout. After all, what could we possibly have that the king would need or even want?

No. Jesus calls only to offer us the privilege of joining his retinue. He extends to us the singular honor of following in his train, of suffering (for a time), of dying (which we will do anyhow), of joining him and a host of others—mighty as an army with banners—in glorious resurrection.